Young Photographer

John Craven and John Wasley

Young Photographer

EP Publishing Limited

ISBN 0 7158 0667 X (LIMP)
ISBN 0 7158 0813 3 (CASED)

Published by EP Publishing Ltd,
East Ardsley, Wakefield, West
Yorkshire, 1981

Cover photos and photos on pp. 10
and 17 by Ian Wood, Leicester.

All other photography by John
Wasley.

Design by Douglas Martin
Associates.

Text photoset in 11/13pt Morges
and printed by G. Beard & Son Ltd,
Brighton, Sussex. Bound in Great
Britain by Seawhite Ltd.

Contents

On holiday, everyone takes pictures of everything they can see. While you are shooting, remember the other happy snappers. Sometimes they make good subjects in themselves. To capture them though, you must have your camera with you all the time, and make sure it is ready for instant picture-taking.

Introduction

1
Making a start

People have always thought in pictures. Ever since human beings first recorded their thoughts and observations, pictures have played a vital part. The earliest writing, for instance, was in the form of pictograms or hieroglyphs, and even today languages such as Chinese and Japanese are written in the form of stylised pictures. So photography is just a modern version of a very old human habit.

The marvellous thing about photography is that anyone can join in. In the past, you had to have a talent for drawing or painting to make pictures, and the time to do it. That's why so few people were really able to create a record in pictures of what was happening around them. The camera has changed all that, making it possible for almost anyone to capture that 'moment frozen in time' which is a photograph.

That does not mean, of course, that photography is not an art. Most people who take 'snaps' are not photographers as such: what they want to do is to look back later at the high spots of a holiday, or a visit to a famous place, or an important moment for their family. Some of the photographs may be blurred or wrongly exposed, but they will still have a place in the albums. However, when you take up photography as a hobby, your purposes are rather different. It then becomes a way of expressing yourself, of recording how you as a person see the world about you and the people, events and things in it. You begin to realise that it's a mixture of art, craft and technical know-how, and there is a lot of pleasure to be got from learning how to handle all three.

The human eye is in fact the most perfect lens we know, and if we also had a built-in method of printing the pictures it sees, we wouldn't need cameras. As things are, though, the best we can ao is convert what we see with our eyes into memories—and memory is not nearly as accurate as a photograph. That's why photography is such a useful tool in many other hobbies: for instance, if you are a keen bird-watcher or aircraft spotter, the camera can catch the detail of a fleeting moment of action or movement which would otherwise be lost.

A photograph shows you so much more than you have taken in with your eyes. The eye 'records' the general scene and some details, but there is quite a lot it misses. With photographs, you can study those missed details whenever you want, for as long as you like. And there are some things which only the camera can see. Ultra high speed photography, which can 'see' 1,250 times faster than the wink of an eye, makes it possible to discover exactly what happens to the surface of a pond when a stone hits it, or how a bird moves its wings to hover in the air. The camera can also take a series of photographs of very slow-moving developments, like the growth of a plant, over weeks or even months, and then speed the film up so that it looks as if it had all happened in seconds. These are things which no human eye has ever been able to see, because they happen too slowly or too quickly for our eyes to take in.

These days, making a start in photography involves working your way through a bewildering array of equipment. You can see that as soon as you go into a camera shop, even quite a small one. It's rather like entering Aladdin's cave: there are all the 'treasures' lined up on the shelves, surrounded by a mass of extras and accessories – camera cases, alternative lenses, exposure meters, flash guns, tripod stands, blower brushes, cable releases, cleaning kits. The number of extras you can use with the most basic camera seems endless, and there are countless different makes offering a vast range of features, all of them usually claiming to be the 'best'.

If you are not careful, you can leave the shop loaded down like a pack-horse with all sorts of equipment. At the same time, you'll have a very empty feeling in your pocket. It's a great temptation, of course, to think that the more bits of kit you have, the better your photography is going to be, but this is not true. As the editor of a well-known photography magazine once put it: 'Skill in photography is acquired by practice, and not by purchase.' In other words, it isn't the camera that counts, it's you; your skill and judgement 'composes' a photograph, assesses the lighting, and decides on the angle and moment at which a picture should be taken. All the camera does is make a record, and as long as it is a reputable make and good of its kind, it does not matter very much which camera it is. The extras and the automatic features do, of course, make photography a lot easier: with telephoto or zoom lenses, for instance, you can take pictures from a distance which the ordinary standard lens could never handle. Even so, there is no substitute for a photographer's own skill and talent, and some of the most beautiful photographs ever taken were done with very simple, and even very crude equipment.

When I went along to talk photography with a professional, Ralph Lewis, I discovered that he began as a boy, with the simplest of simple cameras. 'It cost about 1s. 6d. [7½p] from Woolworth's,' he recalls. 'It had a wire frame as a viewfinder and the lens looked like the bottom of a beer bottle. Even so, I could still get the photographs I wanted with it. Basically, I aim to take the same sort of pictures today, though naturally my equipment is infininitely more sophisticated.'

Ralph told me that from the very start he was attracted to landscape photography and interesting buildings, and today his work appears in books, encyclopedias and other publications. Like many photographers, Ralph took his inspiration from a great artist. In his case, the artist was John Constable, the famous English landscape painter. 'Constable and other really brilliant artists knew an enormous amount that is important to photographers,' said Ralph in his studio near London. 'They knew about composition, balance, the effects of light, giving depth and definition to a subject. Above all, they knew how to make a picture tell a story – or to put it another way, how to make it have some meaning and get across information about the subject.'

If you think about it, some of Constable's paintings make you almost feel the warmth of the sun and smell the bales of hay. 'That's just the sort of feeling you should get from a landscape photograph,' Ralph said. 'And the best way to learn how to do it is to start with a simple, basic camera.'

Did that mean no technological aids or automation? The answer was 'Yes', to start with. 'Don't think I disapprove of automation in photography – I'm all in favour of it,' Ralph emphasised. 'Automatic focusing or automatic exposures are marvellous aids for photography. But to begin with, photographers must learn how to perform the functions which have now been automated or they may never know what the camera is doing. For instance, before you use automatic focusing for taking photographs, you ought to know how to focus the camera yourself. The simpler a first camera is, the easier it is to learn the art of photography – and the more thoroughly you'll learn it, too.'

Beginners, Ralph also thinks, should ideally start processing and developing their own photographs at the same time. Again, the rule is to start with the basics, developing contact prints to begin with. Later, you can start using an enlarger, just as, later, you can go on to a more sophisticated camera. 'I would say that a basic 35mm camera makes a good first camera,' Ralph told me. 'Afterwards, photographers can go on to coupled rangefinder cameras, and as they become more skilled, they can start using a variety of different lenses.'

That reminded me of a saying the Romans used to have: *Festina lente* ('hasten slowly'), and it seemed a good principle to apply to photography. It helps, too, if you gain as much experience as possible in doing different sorts of photography. 'It's a good way to discover what you're best at, and what you like doing best. That's very often the same thing,' was Ralph Lewis's comment.

The range of subjects to photograph is very wide – as wide as the world, in fact. Pictorial or landscape photography, living creatures, plants, trees and flowers, transport of various kinds – aeroplanes, cars, buses, trains – sports, buildings and people – the scope is endless.

'What about the film in the camera?' I asked.

'Well, faster film can be used in a greater variety of lighting,' Ralph advised. 'But one thing is particularly important, and that is using black and white film to start with. With black and white photographs it's much easier to see what you've got. You can examine a black and white photo with a magnifying glass to check on definition and grain, for instance.' There are several other advantages, too. Black and white film gives you greater scope in exposure times for taking and processing photographs. You have to be very precise with the length of exposure you use, and black and white gives you the chance to be precise. It also has the advantage of being 10 to 15 per cent cheaper than colour film.

When the times comes to examine your photograph, you will need to know just what you did to get that particular result – so make a habit of writing down the details of each shot you take: the object or scene or subject; the lighting conditions, for instance dark foreground, light sky; how far you were from the object or scene when you took the photographs; the length of exposure; and any other information that will tell you how your camera worked in specific conditions. Don't rely on your memory.

It is also a good idea to look at the pictures taken by other photographers, and to work out the angle from which they were taken, and where the light source was situated. You can make your own library of pictures by cutting them out of magazines, and keep them by you for reference.

My visit to Ralph Lewis gave me five rules for making a good start in photography, so let's sum up:

Rule 1	Learn as much as you can about composition, light and shade, and perspective, by looking at the works of painters and other artists.
Rule 2	Start simple when you take your first photographs, using a basic camera in which the processes have to be done by hand.
Rule 3	Experiment to discover what you do best.
Rule 4	Use black and white film to start with, to show you precisely what you have done in a photograph, and make notes at the time so you have a record of how you did it.
Rule 5	Make a collection of good photographs, and use them for study and reference.

Buying a camera

Graham Thom owns a busy photographic equipment shop. He has been a photography enthusiast for as long as he can remember and has been selling camera equipment for the past eleven years. The young enthusiast is no stranger to Graham. The first thing he checks up on, he told me, is whether photography is just a passing craze or is likely to be a serious hobby.

'It's not difficult to find that out,' Graham said with a smile. 'I simply ask them what sort of photography they want to do. If the answer is taking photographs of the family, or taking a camera on holiday, then the youngster wants a camera, not a hobby.'

So, what sort of an answer is he looking for? 'The answer that says the youngster concerned intends to be creative with a camera,' was Graham's reply. 'He or she might say they want to take pictures of buildings, or animals, or landscapes. They may want to take family pictures as well, of course, but their interest goes further than that.'

'You can also tell how serious youngsters are by how they react to cameras,' Graham went on. 'I might offer them two cameras – a 110 automatic and a better, possibly more expensive, single lens reflex camera. If they start asking questions about the better camera, then you know they're genuinely keen on photography.'

Like Ralph Lewis, Graham Thom favours the 35mm camera as a good first camera. It allows you to adjust light values and experiment with exposures and depth of focus, and later on you can use it with different lenses and colour as well as black and white.

11

What about money, though? A good camera might be expensive for a youngster. 'For a youngster, yes, it could well be,' Graham agreed. 'Usually they come here with about £10 or £20 which they have saved, and expect to buy a camera with that. Well, of course, you can buy a camera in this price range, but not the sort of camera you need if you're going to learn photography. So, I tell them to come back when they have got about £50.'

That could sound like a fortune, but Graham reckons that the genuine enthusiast won't be put off by having to save for a while. A youngster who just wants a camera will buy one of the cheaper, cassette-loading ones, and be very happy with it.

When it comes to cassette films, Graham often has to explain the drawbacks as far as the young photographer is concerned. 'In photography, using cassette films means there are certain things you can't do. Cassettes normally produce colour prints. Black and white cassettes are limited, and you often can't take slides at all.'

'The trouble is,' Graham went on, 'that there's a fallacy that loading film into a camera by hand is difficult, if not impossible. People have told me that the film gets tangled when you load it by hand, or you can't get it properly attached at the end of the spool. It's not true at all.'

Graham went on to explain his own method of making sure the film is loaded properly. It is quite simple. Once you have loaded the film, wind on to take up the slack with the rewind crank, and then rotate the transport lever. If the film has been loaded correctly, then the rewind crank will turn in the opposite direction.

Graham Thom is willing to spend some time explaining all this to his young customers because he is one of those shop-keepers who wants to make sure that his customers know what they are buying, and how to use it. 'If you find a retailer who just dumps a few cameras on the counter and lets you get on with choosing one of them yourself, then he's not really interested in you as a photographer,' Graham advised. 'He just wants to sell you a camera. Ideally, a retailer should be your friend and adviser on a long-term basis.' As long as you don't try to talk to him at length about your camera and your photographs at a busy time – like Saturday mornings, or the last few days before Christmas – he should be glad to spend time with you and answer your questions. Try going after school – photographic shops are open for quite a while after that, and it is normally a fairly quiet time.

Once you have bought your camera, though, you should resist the temptation to load it with film straight away and rush out to start taking pictures. It is better to have a 'dry run' – that is, using the camera without a film in it. And do read the instructions carefully – twice, and more often if necessary.

'You should also get to know your camera and all its controls until you can "see" them with your eyes shut,' Graham advised. 'If you're out in the street with your camera and something suddenly happens which you want to photograph, you won't have time to search for the shutter lever. Your finger should reach for it automatically. In fact, you should be able to operate your camera without thinking about it – the thing you should concentrate on completely is taking the picture.'

It's a good habit to have your camera ready for use at a moment's notice when you're out and about. The camera should be set for action, but to avoid taking pictures by mistake, keep the shutter lock on. However, if something occurs suddenly, don't get so excited you forget to unlock it.

Local newspapers – and even national ones sometimes – rely on members of the public for dramatic pictures of events which happen unexpectedly – pictures which their staff photographers can't take, because they aren't there. Remember you may be the only person around who has a camera – and if the event is important enough, you might see your picture – and your name – on the front page!

Photography is one of the small number of hobbies which can lead to a professional job, so having talked about sending photographs to newspapers, I asked Graham how people got into photography as a living. How did *he* start? 'I went to work in a photographic shop,' Graham told me. 'Just by handling and selling the equipment, and talking about it to customers, you can learn a great deal about cameras and accessories; in fact you can learn a lot about photography generally.'

Graham went on to suggest that you might try asking your local photographic shop if there are any part-time jobs available in the school holidays, or on busy Saturday mornings. Or you could keep an eye on job advertisements in the local paper to see if there are any jobs of that sort mentioned there.

What about full-time training, once would-be photographers have left school? There is the old-fashioned way – going to work in a photographic studio, making tea or sweeping the floor or delivering films – anything and everything even if it is a bit humdrum for a start. The important thing is that you will be able to learn about cameras, processing, lighting and other photographic techniques. 'A general photographic studio is the best place for that sort of training,' said Graham. 'A studio that handles most assignments – such as brochures for industrial or commercial firms, weddings, advertising and so on.'

Of course, training in photography can be of the more formal kind as well. There are some very good college courses available, and you can learn about these from your local Careers Centre. The City and Guilds courses, which are the basic qualification for many photographic jobs, last two years, full-time. However, you can also take the courses by studying in the evenings. They include one on General Photography (No. 744) and another on Scientific and Technical Photography (No. 745); there are also advanced courses and separate courses in colour retouching and special techniques. Normally, the basic qualifications to undertake a City and Guilds course are 'A' levels in Mathematics, English and a Science.

However, don't think that you have to be a genius or another Cartier-Bresson or David Bailey to take up a career in photography. If you are – fine! If not, then remember there are thousands of photographers hard at work every day in commercial studios, industrial and commercial firms, hospitals, museums, laboratories and government departments. If you have a yen for action, you could consider becoming a newspaper photographer – first on your local newspaper and later, if you are lucky, on a national paper.

How photography began

Photography – or at least the principles behind it – is a lot older than you might think. As early as 1000 A.D., a device called the *camera obscura* – Latin for 'dark room' – was known. This was a darkened room which had a small hole in the window shutter; light from a brightly lit scene outside came in through the hole and formed a picture on the surface opposite the hole – though unfortunately the image was projected upside down!

In the sixteenth century, Italian inventors began to put the *camera obscura* into roughly the basic form of the camera as we know it today. Geronimo Cardano suggested that a convex lens would produce a brighter image, and in 1573 Ignazio Danti discovered that he could turn the image formed in the *camera obscura* the right way up by using a concave mirror behind the lens. Later on came methods of enlarging or reducing the image, and it became possible to use a small dark box instead of the darkened room.

By the eighteenth century, the *camera obscura* was being widely used, especially by painters sketching natural scenes,

The idea of changing the size of the image in the camera is something we take for granted today, but as long ago as the sixteenth century scientists made experiments in this direction.

since the image could be projected onto a sheet of paper and used as the basis for the sketch. It was very useful – but it had one big drawback. There was, as yet, no way in which the image seen in the *camera obscura* could be fixed, so that it could be studied or used for reference at any time.

'Fixing the image' was finally achieved by a Frenchman, Joseph Nicephore Niepce. Niepce was a chemist who set out on a painstaking series of experiments, testing a wide range of materials for sensitivity to light. He discovered that bitumen hardened when exposed to light, and in 1822 he finally produced the first permanent photograph as a transparent image on glass. Four years later, Niepce obtained a photograph on a pewter plate which was the first to be taken from nature. It was taken from the upper-storey window of Niepce's house at Gras, near Châlon-sur-Saône in north-east France, and shows a summer view of the court-yard, with a pigeon-house, a pear tree, a bakehouse, a barn and a wing of the house on the right of the picture. Niepce had to expose his plate for eight hours. When the image was fixed on the plate, the plate was washed with a mixture of oil of lavender and white petroleum: this dissolved away the parts of the bitumen on the plate which had not been hardened by the light. The resulting picture was a permanent direct positive.

The method Niepce used was called heliography or printing by sunlight and though it was obviously successful, the great length of time required for the exposure was a problem. To solve it, Niepce joined forces with a painter called Louis Jacques Mande Daguerre, who had been experimenting with photography for several years. Niepce and Daguerre worked together from 1829 until Niepce's death in 1833, seeking ways to improve the heliographic process. They tested several materials for light sensitivity, and first tried coating silver plates with silver salts. Later, they turned their attention to silver iodide. After Niepce's death, Daguerre, continuing alone, discovered in 1839 that it was possible to fix an image by exposing an iodized silver plate in a camera.

The successful result Daguerre had been seeking happened, ironically, after he had gone home in a huff because the weather was not suitable for exposing his plates. The day was sunny when he started out, but after he had exposed one plate clouds blew across the sky and blotted out the sun. In disgust, Daguerre packed up his equipment, including the plate, and abandoned the outing. Next day, he was just setting off to try again when he looked at the plate that had been exposed the previous day. To his amazement and delight, the plate was not blank or blurred, as he

15

THE FIRST FIFTY YEARS

October 1839

First studio portrait taken in New York

March 1840

First photographic portrait studio opened in New York. It was advertised as 'the first daguerreotype gallery for portraits' and exposure time for pictures was between three and five minutes

March 1841

First photographic studio in Britain opened. In order to get subjects to sit still for the long exposure time, they had to have their heads clamped into an iron collar. As a reward, however, they were given their photographs five minutes after this painful session came to an end

1858

The first aerial photograph was made by the French 'aeronaut' Gaspard Felix Tournachon from a balloon 262ft above a Paris suburb

1861

The first colour transparency made in Britain: a picture of a tartan ribbon bow against a black velvet background

1869

First colour transparency made in Paris, showing a rainbow

1881

The first photographic camera film to be produced were the packets of 12 manufactured by Alfred Pumphrey of Birmingham. They came in various sizes, from 3.25 x 4.25ins to 8 x 10ins

1887

Hannibal Goodwin invented the modern transparent roll film

1888

The Kodak camera, the first portable roll film camera, was produced by the Eastman Dry Plate Company of Rochester, New York. Called 'Kodak' because the name sounded like the click of a camera shutter, Kodak No. 1 produced circular 2.5in diameter prints

1889

Eastman Company marketed first commercial celluloid roll films

expected, but showed an image of the scene he thought the weather had made impossible.

It was success at last for Daguerre, but why? Unless he knew that, he might not be able to produce an image again. The explanation, he discovered, was a jar of mercury in his cupboard: Daguerre had left the container open and the mercury fumes had brought out the image on the plate. This image could be fixed with the most ordinary of materials – a solution of common salt. Daguerre's photographic process was the one which made photography a commercial proposition, and the advances he had made by 1839 had reduced the time for exposure of photographs from eight hours to between fifteen and thirty minutes. When the details were announced in Paris, in August 1839, they created a sensation and immediately started a craze. The hobby of 'daguerreotyping', as it was called, became the rage. According to a German living in Paris at the time: 'A few days later, you could see in all the squares of Paris three-legged dark-boxes planted in front of churches and palaces.'

By September, the first commercial camera went on sale in Paris. Daguerre provided the specifications, and the camera was fitted with an achromatic (colour free) lens by the optician Charles Chevalier. The camera was made of wood and measured 267 x 311 x 368mm when closed. The firm of Alphonse Giroux, who marketed it, were the world's first photographic dealers.

The picture Daguerre had produced by accident in 1839 was a positive, which meant that it could not be copied. The photograph negative, from which copies could be taken, had, however, already arrived. In February 1839 came the announcement of the negative-positive process developed by the English scientist, William Henry Fox Talbot. Fox Talbot fixed reversed prints on silver paper; and with this 'Calotype process' as he called it, he could print as many copies as he wanted of the pictures he named 'photogenic drawings'.

Fox Talbot was only the first of many experimenters who gradually improved photography so that by the time of the American Civil War (1861-65) it could be used to make a documentary record for the first time.

George Eastman (1895-1932) laid the foundations of photography as a hobby for all. Apart from the Kodak camera, his company provided the first daylight loading black-paper-backed roll film in 1894, the first panchromatic film in 1914, and Kodachrome in 1935. And the process still goes on, with new and exciting improvements appearing year by year.

4
Travelling with a camera

There can't be many people who don't pack a camera as part of their holiday luggage, especially if they are going abroad. But if you want your holiday photographs to be a cut above the average snapshots, there are certain preparations you should make.

First of all, think about the area where you're going. Does it have places of special interest you will want to photograph? Will you go on any excursions where you will want to use your camera? Reckoning up like this will give a good idea of how much film you should take with you. If you are going abroad, remember you may not be able to buy the film you are used to using, or if you can, it may be very expensive. It's much better, in any case, to take too much film than too little. There is nothing worse than desperately wanting to 'shoot' something with an empty camera. If you get home with unused rolls of film still in your bag, you can always use them later, and nothing is lost.

Next, do make sure your camera is working properly. Check it yourself, or send it to a dealer or the manufacturer to do it for you. The same, of course, applies to all the equipment you plan to take with you, if you have reached the stage of using alternative lenses and other accessories. It is vital, for instance, that your light meter is accurate: over- or under-exposure due to a faulty light meter can ruin pictures.

Checking equipment before you leave is particularly important because you will be taking photographs for one, two or even three weeks without having any film processed: if there is anything wrong with your camera, you won't know until you start processing the film. There will be cries of despair from the darkroom then – so avoid as much of this frustration as you can by getting everything thoroughly checked over and any faults corrected in good time.

If, by any chance, you are thinking of taking a new camera with you on holiday, do get acquainted with it before you go. Run at least one roll of film through it, just to make sure you can handle it easily and it operates properly.

Protect your camera and equipment from possible damage. On a beach, cameras and lenses are always at risk from salt water and sand. Before you leave home, cover your camera in a plastic bag and cut a hole in the side so that you can slip the lens through when the time comes to take a picture. The bag should be soft enough for you to operate the controls through it; if not, you have probably put it on too tightly.

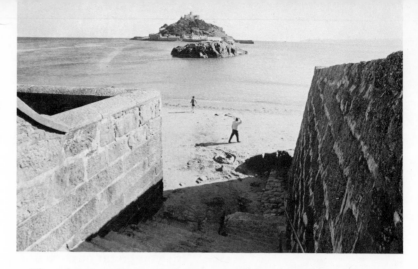

The plastic will protect your precious lens from sand and from salt water splashes. However, if you do get sand on the lens or, in fact, on the camera at all, don't ever wipe it off with a rubbing motion. Sand can make scratches on lenses, or filters, and you may have to buy replacements. So, blow the sand off or shake the camera gently, and if any sand remains after that, try flicking it off with the end of a handkerchief. This helps to minimise any damage done by the sand, though it is still possible that sand has got inside the camera; if so, it may jam the moving parts.

It's inadvisable, to say the least, to drop your camera in the sea. Always carry it round your neck or your wrist by a strap, and if you go into the water, wade out slowly and carefully to make sure you do not stumble and get a ducking. You may be drip dry, but your camera is not, and if enough salt water gets into it, it can rust up completely. If the worst happens, then retrieve the camera as quickly as possible, and put it in a bucket of fresh water. Only a camera dealer will be able to tell you if it can be repaired or not, but either way you will be without your camera for the rest of the holiday; so take care.

Touring holidays or photographing during excursions and sightseeing can lead to another set of problems. When photographs do not turn out satisfactorily, it is usually due to incorrect exposure or 'camera shake'. In fact, these reasons account for nine out of ten of photograph failures. Setting the correct exposure is a matter between you and your camera, but 'camera shake' is not always easy to avoid. If you want to take a photograph from a moving train, aircraft or car, avoid leaning your elbows on anything. If you do, then you will vibrate along with the vehicle, and so will your camera. Much better to use your muscles to hold yourself steady, and tuck your elbows against your waist. Try to avoid taking pictures through a vehicle window, whether moving or stationary, if there are likely to be reflections in the window which will show up on your picture. If you are standing up in a moving vehicle and taking a picture, relax your knees, and brace your elbows against you to help hold the camera steady.

When you progress to using extra lenses, you will find that these can be quite heavy, so you may have difficulty holding your camera steady enough. The answer is a bean bag which you can mould round your lens or camera to hold it against a window frame, or the branch of a tree, or wherever you want to rest it. The bag will also protect your camera from getting scratched.

You can make a bean bag yourself, from a cloth bag measuring about 30 x 20cm. It should have a zip along one edge, and be filled with dried peas or beans. You can get these from most supermarkets or health food shops. (Don't be tempted to use sand as a filling, for the reasons I talked about earlier in this section.) If the weight of the bag is a problem because you are travelling by air, take the empty bag and buy something to fill it with when you get there – the local market should be able to provide what you need.

And don't cram the bag too full. This will make it much too hard and resistant. Fill it loosely, so that it is flexible and you can mould it round the lens or camera. It will hold your lens very firmly, but do remember to brace yourself as you release the camera shutter.

After a day out with your camera, particularly if you have been on an excursion or a beach, make sure you give your camera and lenses a thorough clean. Remember that one speck of sand or the grit from a dusty road is quite enough to scratch an entire roll of film if it gets caught in the film pressure plate. If possible, try to finish a roll of film by the end of the day, so that you can open the camera in the evening and give it a good clean. If you are in a particularly hot country, wiping the lens clean with tissues or a handkerchief won't be satisfactory: static is created and all you are doing is pushing the dirt on the lens from one side to the other. Better to use a soft paintbrush and flick the dust away with gentle movements. Blowing dust and grit or sand out is the best idea of all, and for this, remember to take a rubber blower with you.

Air-conditioned rooms in hot countries are wonderful for people, but they can spell disaster for your camera and your films unless you're careful. Air-conditioning units tend to create a damp atmosphere and unless you can keep your films and your camera dry at night in well-sealed bags, the damp can ruin your photographs. Once film becomes damp enough to stick together, that is the end of it. So, never put your camera, film or equipment near the air-conditioning unit in your room: choose the dryest place you can find – a drawer, or the bottom of a cupboard, or even the floor.

At the same time, do not go to the other extreme and leave your camera or lenses lying about in the sun. The lens, after all, is a magnifying glass and concentrates the sun's rays, so that you could find the inside of your camera has been burned out.

At the start of the day, check your list of equipment to make sure you have everything you need. If you find yourself halfway up a mountain without a long lens, for instance, and there's a fine valley spread out below you, there will be nothing you can do about it. And remember to take flash bulbs or an electronic flash if you are going to be visiting caves or temples with dark interiors.

Photographing by the sea or at high altitudes can present special problems because of the excess of blue light that can exist there. The solution here is an ultra-violet or UV lens. This reduces the amount of blue light, and so improves colour rendering. The finished photograph will then look more natural. If you have reached the stage where you are using more than one lens, you could fit a UV filter to each one. As well as reducing the 'blue', these filters protect your lens and are not nearly so expensive to replace.

Do make a few brief notes for each roll of photographs taken. A small notebook will be fine for writing down 'captions' – details which remind you which scene or building is which when you get home and start sorting through the developed photographs.

Finally, there's one very important thing you have to bear in mind, particularly if you are travelling in Eastern Europe or the Middle East. That is that photography can get you into big trouble. From time to time you see in the newspapers that a holiday-maker in Russia, perhaps, has been arrested for taking 'illegal' photographs, usually of military installations or perhaps military planes at airports. It's no joke, and it could happen to you. Anyway, in most cases the only value of the photograph will be that it was 'forbidden'. (The photograph on the left was allowed because the rocket was on show at an air day.)

There are also people in some parts of the world who are very superstitious about having their photographs taken. In some Middle Eastern countries, for instance, people may think you are 'stealing their souls' with your camera lens. Don't insult them by clicking away: it may sound strange to you, but they believe it. And you could find your camera smashed or confiscated.

At the other extreme, there are some people who know the

appeal to photographers of their native costumes and picturesque surroundings. They not only want you to take their photographs, but expect to be paid for it. If you are willing to pay up, first get their permission, and have some money handy.

5
The world of photography

Most hobbies have their own special 'worlds' with clubs, publications, books and sometimes even special holidays for enthusiasts. It is perfectly natural that people with the same hobby or interest should want to exchange news and views and 'talk shop', and photography is no exception.

This swapping of information can be very valuable, and as soon as you are old enough – say about fifteen or sixteen – you should think about joining your local camera club, if there is one. Many clubs offer family membership, so if your parents are keen, you can go along too.

Most clubs have a wide variety of events. For instance, there are exhibitions where members get the chance to put their work on display. There are also club competitions, and inter-club competitions, which you should enter as soon as you can. Camera clubs may also have visiting speakers, who are often very experienced amateurs or maybe professionals – and you can pick up a lot of good tips from them, and get answers to any problems you have come up against.

There are also a large number of photography magazines, with articles covering a wide range of topics, and advertisements and advice on the latest equipment. These publications often run competitions which are well worth entering, because of the fun and the challenge. Of course, you will be competing with a vast number of other photographers, but as long as you stick to the rules of the competition and turn out good entries, you will have as much chance of success as all the others. When it comes to competitions, though, do read the rules very carefully: they are usually in small print and you should make sure you understand every word of them. Otherwise, you may find yourself disqualified. Watch out for competitions which don't send your pictures back to you, or which claim the copyright on them. Don't enter – because what you could be doing, in effect, is giving away your photographs. Most photography competitions have set subjects, such as 'The British at leisure' or 'Wild life in Britain', and some have several categories.

You may already have in your store of photographs prints which would make suitable entries, or you may want to take

21

photographs specially for the competition. Sometimes, the rules call for a *series* of photographs – and that is worth bearing in mind when you are taking pictures which might be useful for some future contest.

It is not just photographic magazines which run competitions – lots of newspapers and other magazines have them as well, particularly in the summer months when holidays and holiday photographs are on many people's minds. Remember, you can usually see these in your local library.

You might also find it useful and interesting to go to photographic exhibitions. These are mounted in galleries or museums and take place all over the country. In one week in the autumn of 1978, for instance, there were no less than 28 photographic exhibitions going on at the same time, and a month earlier there were 33. These exhibitions were shown in Aberdeen, Accrington, Birmingham, Kendal, Nottingham, Oxford, York, Cheltenham, and several other towns, as well as in London. So, it is quite possible that there could be an exhibition you are able to reach without difficulty from your home town. Your local council can be a source of information about local exhibitions, and so can your public library.

As you browse among the photographs, you'll see just what can be achieved by what was once called the Magic Box. It's a good name, because I often think that magical things happen when a camera is in the hands of someone who really understands what it can do.

I have spent most of my working life alongside photographers and television camera crews, and I learnt very early on that their best pictures are far more powerful than any words that I can write. On some assignments, they have been deeply moved by the images they have seen down their viewfinders, and have passed on that emotion – through their pictures – to millions of readers and viewers.

And whether they are painstakingly setting up a studio shot, or keeping pace with a fast-moving news story, photographers are artists in action. Myself? I'm just a 'happy snapper', using my camera to capture personal memories of interesting places and special moments with my family. Over the years, I've picked up quite a few tips from my camera-toting friends but I would never claim to be in their highly-talented league.

Whether you hope to be a professional photographer some day, or just want to get the best possible use and *fun* from your camera as an enthusiastic amateur, I hope that the rest of this book will help you on your way.

Chapter One

The Tools

1

The camera and the lens

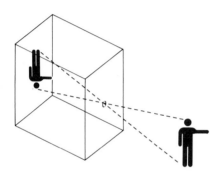

The pinhole camera principle

Have you ever been in a dark room and seen the sunlight streaming through the keyhole to the wall opposite to form an upside down image of what is outside? Well, that is essentially what a camera does.

If you fixed a piece of light-sensitive material at the point where the image is formed and processed it, you would get a picture. The pioneers in photography back in the 1800s did that, only they had a box with a tiny hole in one side and called it the pinhole camera.

The only problem was, each exposure took such a long time. They enlarged the hole to get more light, but the bigger they made it the less distinct the image became. Then someone discovered that if a piece of specially shaped glass was fixed in front of the hole, it collected the rays and bent them to sharpen the image at the plane where the light-sensitive material – the film – was situated.

Viewfinder camera

35mm single lens reflex

Twin lens reflex

120 single lens reflex

Camera '80

From those two simple steps, the camera has leapt ahead to become the sophisticated instrument it is today – in all its varieties. However, it can be broken down basically into two categories. There are those which permit image viewing through optically correct glass set in the top of the camera, and those which permit viewing direct through the lens.

The first, known as a viewfinder camera, is commonly found among the less expensive variety – the cartridge load, instamatic type. But there are some more sophisticated models which tend to be automated, sometimes even to the focusing. This category of camera usually has a special mirror system built in to the viewfinder to enable you to find the range. You usually see a double or split image in the viewfinder which must be merged into one.

The other type of camera is called the reflex. One, fast losing ground, collects and focuses the image through a lens set above the one used for making the picture. Thus, it is called a twin lens reflex (TLR). The image is formed on a silvered plate or mirror set at an angle behind the lens. It passes the image on upwards to a horizontal ground glass screen in the top of the camera, the same size as the film. Since you have to look down at this image, it has earned the name of 'waist level viewfinder'. The mirror does turn the image the right way up, but it is reversed. This can be a bit confusing in moments of panic because you have to move the camera in the opposite direction to that seen in the ground glass. So, for action photography, there is a hole cut in the stand-up, light-stopping hood. Called a 'sports finder', it permits direct viewing.

With the exception of a couple of notables, the TLR has largely given way to the single lens reflex (SLR). This is designed with a viewing system which takes the image seen right through the taking lens. Again, an angled mirror collects and deflects the image upwards. However, as it is

Double image rangefinder

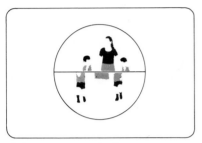

Split image rangefinder

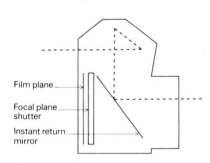

Film plane

Focal plane
shutter

Instant return
mirror

SLR principle

positioned just in front of the film, it has to flip up during exposure to let the light reach the film, and then back into place right afterwards. The instant return mirror does lose the image for the duration of the exposure but after a while you hardly notice it.

Most SLRs have prisms set on the top which turn the image the right way round and allow eye level viewing. Usually they are fixed, but one or two can be removed for waist level viewing. Some also have rangefinders. These are not essential though, because the image is made sharp by the act of focusing.

Formats

The vast majority of amateurs use roll film. Roll films come in four sizes – 120, 35mm, 126, and 110. The last two are cartridge loaded films.

On 120 film, you can shoot (depending on the camera) image sizes of 6cm by 7, 6, or 4.5cm. 35mm usually produces an image size of 36mm by 24mm but one or two cameras halve it to 36mm by 12mm. 126 images are 28mm square, and 110, 13mm by 17mm. All of them have to be enlarged to produce a photograph of a reasonable size.

Since a larger negative requires less enlargement they generally give better quality pictures, size for size. So, apart from spies, serious cameramen try to stick with 35mm and upwards. Nevertheless, it is possible to buy just about any type of camera in any format. The TLR is the exception, which is available mainly for 120 sizes, adapting, in one or two cases, to 35mm.

Lenses

Every camera has a standard lens which generally gives you the same view and normal eyesight. As this is decided by the diagonal of the film format, it follows that bigger cameras require a bigger standard lens.

On some cameras, notably the SLR, lenses can be changed. This allows you to magnify or shrink the image size. The amount of magnification is decided by the angle of view of the lens which, in turn is defined by the focal length. This, to all intents and purposes, is the distance between the centre of the lens and the film. These days it is measured in millimetres.

Thus, the 35mm camera has a standard lens of around 50mm, while on 120 it is about 80mm. However, rather than discuss each camera format every time a focal length is mentioned, we will here stick to the most popular – 35mm.

If you wanted to double the image size, you would pick a telephoto lens of 100mm – that is twice the standard of 50mm. If you wanted to halve it, you would use a 25mm. There are, of course, many others. The favourite telephoto is, for instance, 135mm, and they go on up to 200mm (4X magnification), 500 (10X magnification), and 1000mm (20X magnification) – and all focal lengths in between.

There is another device available which fits behind an ordinary lens and doubles or trebles its focal length. Called a tele-converter, or extender, it is much less expensive than a prime lens. However, a major disadvantage is that light transmission to the film is reduced drastically, and longer exposures than normal are required.

A favourite wide angle lens is the 28mm but they range from 35mm on down through such focal lengths as 25mm, 20mm, 18mm, 9mm, and so on. The image formed by these lenses appears natural down to about 18mm. After that point, straight lines, especially at the edges, are bowed outwards in barrel shapes. This becomes extreme in the very short focal lengths where an angle of view of 180° is crammed into the viewfinder in the form of a circular image.

The zoom

This lens is a firm favourite among photographers. It is designed to provide a variety of image sizes by changing the focal length. You do that by rotating or sliding a ring which may or may not be separate from the focusing ring.

Zoom lenses are available in four categories – wide angle zooms, wide to short telephoto, medium telephoto zooms, and the long telephoto range. Their great advantage is that you

The great advantage of the zoom lens is that you can choose a focal length which suits the subject precisely.

can shoot at a variety of focal lengths without having to spend time changing lenses. Also, they do not confine you to arbitrary lens sizes. You can fill the frame precisely for creative composition right there in the camera.

There is one final item, closely linked to lenses, which should be mentioned: the lens hood. On most lenses, the front element is so far forward in the mount that it picks up stray light rays coming in at odd angles. This causes flare, the result of which is a flat image. All sharpness and contrast disappears. Head them off with a lens hood and the improvement is dramatic. Don't take a chance. Use one for *every* picture you shoot.

Light and film

Light makes a photograph possible. Indeed, the word 'photography' comes from two Greek words: *phos* meaning light, and *graphos*, meaning to paint or draw. When put together, 'photography' makes 'to paint or draw with light'. You would

not be able to make pictures if the light rays did not travel in straight lines. Indeed, you could not even see straight. If its direction of travel were unpredictable, solid objects would not be easily identifiable; worse, you would not be able to guarantee that they were where you see them to be.

Travel is the right word for light, by the way. Light does travel from its source to – well – forever, if nothing gets in its way. And, although it is true that it does travel in straight lines, an actual light ray is wavy. This natural phenomenon makes it easy to measure. All you have to do is find the distance between one wave peak, or crest, and the next. These distances are so small that they are measured in thousand millionths of millimetres, known as nanometres.

A single beam of white light consists of many such wavy lines, all different. Each of these, if they could be seen individually, would appear to be a single colour. You can see these individual colours from time to time in nature as a rainbow, which is nothing more than ordinary daylight 'dissected' for you to see what it is made of.

The spectrum

The miracle of nature which shows us the rainbow is also an important principle of photography. To make use of it, you must physically bend the light ray. That happens when it is passed through a clear medium such as water or glass. It enters as a single colour – white – and emerges out the other side at a different angle and split up into many colours. This is how you can see the rainbow: white light enters tiny water droplets in the air and comes out the other side split up, showing us the beautiful range of colours.

The name given to this bending and dissection of light is refraction. The many colours resulting from refraction is called the spectrum.

The same sort of thing happens in a lens. Remember, the elements are glass – an ideal clear medium. Their purpose is to bend the light rays reflected from the subject you are photographing and bring them into sharp focus on the film. However, as they do, they reveal all the different wavelengths, or colours.

You can see how the spectrum is made up in the diagram opposite. The various wavelengths in nanometres are shown for each colour too. However, it is important to know that this is only a diagram. In real life there are no clear-cut divisions between each colour. It is one continuous flow, each colour gradually giving way to the next and transforming its own colour all the time. Note too, that ultra violet and infra red are

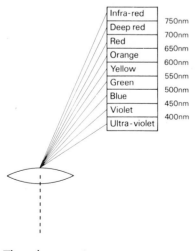

The colour spectrum

included in the diagram. Although you cannot see them, they are included because they both have important parts to play in photography.

While the lens is essential for bringing light rays to a focus point, the act of bending and splitting into the spectrum does produce problems. For instance, blue, when it is refracted to one wavelength (400nm), cannot arrive at the same point of focus as red, which is refracted to 700nm. There is a whole 300nm difference. True, this distance is only tiny, but it is enough to push one or the other out of focus. It is sufficient to make sure that, for instance, a red jacket and a pair of blue jeans on the same person could not be brought into sharp focus at the same time. One or the other would be slightly fuzzy. This problem is known as chromatic aberration.

The answer to this problem is found in passing the entire spectrum through another piece of glass, or lens element. If this second element is introduced behind the first, it reverses the process. It collects all the different wavelengths, bending and reuniting them to make white light once more and, more important, bringing them all to the same, single point of sharp focus. The lens which has been designed to do this is usually labelled 'achromatic'.

Primaries and complementaries

When working in colour or, indeed, black and white, it is easier to 'handle' the spectrum if you boil it down to three broad colour areas. Consider that blue covers 4-500nm; green ranges over 5-600nm; and red spreads itself out over the 6-700nm end. These three are called the primary colours and, when mixed together in equal amounts, they make white light.

However, if you mix only two of the primaries you come up with another colour altogether. This is said to be 'complementary' to the other unmixed primary. Therefore, blue and green make cyan – the complementary of red; green and red give yellow, which complements blue; and blue and red turn up magenta, green's complementary colour.

To digress slightly at this point, you might be interested to know that, in theory, if you mix the three complementary colours together, you get no light at all. While this fact is not so important at this stage, it is useful to bear in mind when you embark on colour printing.

What is important is that you become thoroughly familiar with these colour mixes. They are an essential element of colour composition and you will be working with them often.

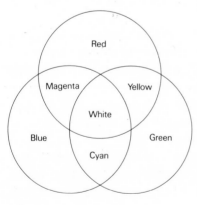

The primary and complementary colours

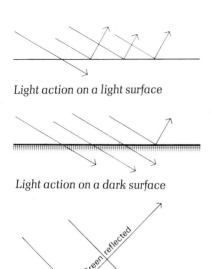

Light action on a light surface

Light action on a dark surface

Green reflected
Blue absorbed
Red absorbed

Light action on green object

Bounced light

Colours in white light are also revealed in another way. You see them when an object bounces back, or reflects, the light striking it. In short, when light hits any object, it is reflected in a different form.

For instance, not as much light is reflected by a black surface as by a light one (see left). This is obvious because in bright sunlight, the former is less painful to look at than the latter. The dark object takes the sting out by absorbing much of the light it receives. White, or light objects, on the other hand, reflect most of the light they receive.

Coloured objects behave in a similar way. This time, however, they absorb and keep some of the colours in the white light striking them and reflect others. So, a leaf, for example, absorbs red and blue and sends to the eye only green.

In practice, it is not as clear-cut as this. To use the leaf as an example again, it can be anything from blue-green to yellow-green. This indicates that some blue, or yellow, respectively is reflected along with the green.

Colour temperature

We have talked a great deal about white light so far. But, in fact, white light can appear in many shades. At midday it is bluish; at sunset it is reddish. Yet they are both known as white light.

Light is formed by and projected from a 'hot body', such as the sun, or a household bulb filament. The colour of this light, however, is determined by the heat of the source. For instance, if you take a piece of iron and, wearing a pair of special heat-resistant gloves, warm it in a forge, it will soon glow red. Heat the iron some more and it will begin to turn white. Increase the heat and the hot end will glow blue.

So, you have three stages of heat: red hot, white hot, blue hot. You can see these colours because they are light. If there were some way of making a 'white' hot poker stay white hot, you could use it as a torch to light your way home in the dark. Indeed, that is what happens in a bulb. The thin metal filament is heated to a certain temperature and kept there so long as it is switched on.

Now, as you can see, there is a direct connection between light, colour, and temperature. As the temperature changes, so does the colour – and *vice versa*. Colour temperature is, however, measured in a special way. It is defined in degrees

9-10000°K	*Heavily overcast*
8000°K	*Hazy*
7000°K	*Light overcast*
6000°K	*Bright sunshine (no clouds)*
5000°K	*Average daylight Blue flash bulbs Electronic flash*
4000°K	*Daylight photofloods 'Cool' white fluorescents*
3000°K	*Photofloods 'Warm' white fluorescents*
2000°K	*Ordinary room light*
1000°K	*Candles*

Colour temperature chart

Kelvin (°K) rather than Centigrade, or even Fahrenheit. The starting point for Kelvin – that is 0 – is equivalent to -273°C.

Using °K right away then, our three poker-heating examples may have produced colour temperatures of 30,000°K (reddish); 60,000°K (white); 90,000°K (bluish).

Degrees Kelvin is important to photography because the various colours of white light produced as the 'temperature' changes affect films in different ways. On black and white film, a low temperature (reddish light) requires slightly more exposure than indicated by your meter.

Of even greater importance is the effect on colour film. These are balanced for specific temperatures. You have daylight films for use in one colour temperature and tungsten films for use in a much lower one. If you try to shoot either film in the wrong light you get all sorts of peculiar colour effects.

Film characteristics

Film is designed to respond to these various reflected wavelengths and colour temperatures, either as colours in colour film, or as shades of grey in black and white film.

A film consists of a gelatine emulsion coated on a clear base. The gelatine is made sensitive to light by 'stirring' in salts of silver bromide, silver chloride, and silver iodide. All together they are generally referred to as silver halides.

When this emulsion is exposed to a subject containing various brightnesses (dark, medium, and light objects reflecting different intensities and colours of light) the lighter ones affect more silver salts in any one area than the darker ones. During development, the more greatly affected areas become blacker and more dense. The dark tones, being affected less, are almost clear. As negatives are viewed by holding them in front of light, the original light tones appear to be darkest on the film, and the original dark tones, light. (see diagram, p. 34).

A colour film is slightly more complex. It has several different emulsion layers, each of which responds to a different colour. In its negative form, not only are the tones reversed, as in a monochrome negative, but so are the colours. They are complementary to the originals. You will see yellow skies, magenta grass, etc.

The silver halides are really too small to see individually in either type of film, except through an extremely powerful microscope. But, during development, they are attracted to one another and tend to clump together. When enough of them get together they become visible in enlarged prints or projected slides and are called grain.

One of the factors which determines the size of grain is the

Grey scale with subject values

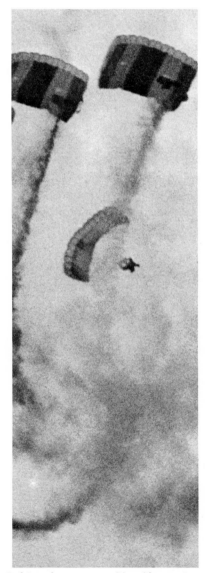

In big enlargements of fast film, grain shows plainly in areas of middle tones.

Glaring surfaces
Specular reflections
Solid highlights

Last presence of texture
Snow in full light
High highlights on skin

Textured bright surfaces
Very light skin in diffused light
Snow side-lit
Light concrete
Bright colours and delicate whites
White skin
Snow in shadow
Light stone

Dark skin
Sunburn
Grey stone
Light foliage
Weathered wood
Dark foliage
Dark stone
Shadows

Black clothing
Leather
Textured shadows

Darkest part of image with detail
First suggestion of texture

Barest tone
Unlit rooms
Shadows in dim light

Empty solid black

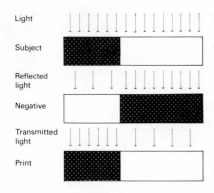

Light

Subject

Reflected light

Negative

Transmitted light

Print

sensitivity of the film. Less sensitive, or slow films, have finer, almost invisible grain. Fast, highly sensitive ones tend to be grainy.

So that you can choose the best one for the type of pictures you have in mind, the sensitivity of films is given on the box. It is indicated in both of the two standard systems of measurement – American Standards Association (ASA) and Deutsche Industrie Norm (DIN). These allow you to work out how much exposure is needed to produce a good image. However, you should choose one system and stick to it. To drive the point home, this book will use only ASA.

There are four film speed categories. Slow, thin emulsion films (50 ASA or less) give extremely fine grain and can record very fine detail, known as a high resolving power. Such films are Ilford Pan F, Kodak Panatomic-X, Efke Adox KB14 and 17.

Medium speed films of 100-200 ASA are most popular for general purpose work. They give fine grain with a reasonable sensitivity and include Ilford FP4, Kodak Plus-X, Efke Adox KB21, and Barfen 125.

In the fast group – around 400 ASA – the grain is larger but the film chemists have managed to make it so fine in recent years that these films are becoming firm favourites among all groups of photographers. The speed permits photography in all kinds of conditions and still produces sharp, detailed, relatively grain-free images. The two great favourites are Ilford HP5 and Kodak Tri-X.

Finally, there are high speed films of 800-1250 ASA. While they have plenty of visible grain, and detail suffers, such films may be the only way out when you are in a photographic corner. Any picture is better than none, and Kodak's Royal-X Pan, or 2475 film, will get it for you.

All that has been said about grain applies to colour too. However, the many emulsion layers tend to hide it. Nevertheless, the multitude of colour films can be fitted into speed categories and will give similar results to those described for black and white.

Films and contrast

Every scene is composed of many brightnesses reflected from the very bright highlights at one end, to deep, dark shadows at the other. The term given to this is the 'brightness range', or contrast. The extent of the brightness range is the difference between the lightest part of the scene and the darkest.

Our eyes can adjust, without our realising it, to both highlights and shadows at the same time. Film is not so capable.

The film's latitude can be used to advantage. Let a messy background 'drop' out the bottom and your main subject then contrasts dramatically against a single dark tone.

Nevertheless, the aim for any picture is to record as much detail in the shadows whilst, at the same time, showing some detail in the highlights. That is where film latitude comes in.

Ideally, a film should be able to record detail in the full highlight/shadow range at the same time – as long as they are not too far apart. Where the brightness range is greater than the film's latitude, detail disappears – blocking up into plain white in the highlights, and/or sinking into unrecorded solid black in the shadows. Slow films are the worst in this respect. They are by nature contrasty, which is to say that they have a limited latitude. Fast films, on the other hand, are able to cope with a great subject contrast easily.

Fast films, then, are most suitable for high contrast situations. While this is true in low light – where the brightness range can be very wide – it is also present in full, unrelieved sunlight. Here you have a problem. A fast film may be too sensitive to use creatively in bright sunlight, whereas the very intensity of everything around you makes the use of slow film easier. It also allows you to take advantage of its fine grain. Somewhere, a compromise has to be found – for instance, medium speed film. That seems to bridge the gap nicely.

Whichever film you decide to make your 'work-horse' you should find out as much as you can about it. If you are going to spend the rest of your photographic life working with one or two films, it will pay you to experiment and discover its limitations and what it can do. This does not mean that you can never use anything else. But it will ensure that you become so familiar with one or two that you do not have to worry about using it and stand much less chance of losing pictures.

Exposure

Exposure is measured as intensity × time. There are two fittings on the camera to handle this; the iris and the shutter.

The iris works just like the one in your eye. How much light actually reaches the film is determined by the size of the aperture made by the iris. On a camera, it is usually a series of overlapping thin metal blades positioned in between the lens elements. You operate it manually by turning a ring on the lens barrel or, on some modern cameras, it is controlled automatically by electronics.

For precise control, the aperture is given a series of numbers, called stops. Each one lets in twice as much light as the next smaller one, and half as much as the next largest. These numbers or stops appear to get smaller as the aperture gets larger. That is because they are fractions of the focal length and only the lower number is given. A typical set are: 1.8, 2, 2.8, 4, 5.6, 8, 11, 16, 22. But, 2 is larger than 22 because they are really f (focal) 1/2 and f1/22. To simplify usage, however, they are known as f2 and f22 – the preceding 'f' denoting the number refers to an aperture.

The shutter

Without the letter 'f' these numbers could be confused with the shutter speed numbers – the other half of the exposure partnership. These numbers are given in fractions of a second – 1/1000th sec., 1/500th, 1/250th, 1/60th, 1/30th, 1/15th, 1/8th, 1/4, 1/2, 1 sec. Each speed, like its aperture partner, admits half as much light as its faster neighbour, and twice as much as its slower one.

You will also find the letter 'B' on the shutter speed dial. It means 'brief time' and indicates that as long as you keep the button pressed, when you have this setting, the shutter willl remain open.

On cameras where the lens is permanently fixed, the shutter is generally a series of overlapping thin metal leaves (just like an iris) and is set between the lens elements. Those cameras with interchangeable lens facilities, however, have their shutter situated within the body, just in front of the film. This one is called a focal plane shutter. It is constructed of rubberised cloth or metal and travels across the film plane, vertically or horizontally. The film is exposed through a variable-sized slit. At speeds up to 1/60th sec. (1/125th sec. on vertically operating shutters) the blinds open fully to expose the entire film frame at once. Above that speed, the slit gets progressively smaller for every faster speed and exposes the film a little at a time.

Using the shutter

Basically, you must try to match the shutter speed to the movement of the subject. If it is too slow, the subject will blur. So, a person sitting requires only 1/30th sec. If he was sprinting, however, you may require 1/250th sec. or even 1/500th sec.

It also controls movement from you. Should you move the camera during exposure, all the picture will be blurred. A fast shutter helps to prevent this. However, much depends on

Match the shutter speed to the subject. The kitten sleeping only required 1/30th sec.; while at play, 1/250th sec. was needed.

the lens. Your original 1/30th sec. might be all right for a standard lens, but a telephoto magnifies camera shake along with the image size. A good rule of thumb is to match the slowest speed you can use with the focal length you are using. Thus a 135mm lens will need at least a shutter of 1/125th sec.

Even then, much depends on how you handle the camera. You must get a firm grip with both hands, and support it in some way if you can. Then, the button must be squeezed gently, not jabbed. The shutter will work just as fast.

Ideal exposure

This is one half of the most vital stage in the entire photographic process. The other is development. When put together properly, the aim is to achieve a negative of reasonable density with a full range of tones (gradation) and/or colours. Most important, just the right amount of light should be permitted to reach the emulsion to indicate a trace of detail in the important shadow and highlight areas.

The average monochrome film is capable of handling a brightness range or contrast ratio of 126:1, or seven stops. Since each greater stop is twice that of its predecessor, it goes: 1, 2, 4, 8, 16, 32, 64, 128 – that is seven stops removed from one. In practical terms it means that you can see detail in a shadow which is seven stops lower in intensity than the brightest detail-revealing highlight. Colour transparency film can only do that, on average, over five stops, or 32:1.

It is possible to reproduce the brightness ratio visually as a series of grey steps. Called a Grey Scale (see page 33), it is solid black at one end and solid white at the other. No detail is expected to show in these extremities.

Exposure meters

To tell us which combination of aperture and shutter speed to use for the correct exposure, we turn to a meter. They are available both separately and built in to the camera. The latter measures either via a separate window, or directly through the lens (TTL). Some operate the settings automatically.

A few meters are powered by the light itself – selenium cell – but the majority are cadmium sulphide (Cds) and are powered by a small battery. Of the two, the Cds is the most sensitive. But it does have two disadvantages. First, it responds differently to some colours than do the film or the eye. Second, it has a memory for light. It will 'recall' the last bright reading taken and inflate the measurement for the next. Thus, you must wait a few seconds for it to settle down.

Averages unlimited

Meters can be used in one of two ways. They will either read the light reflected from the subject, or that falling on it (the incident light).

Most modern meters, particularly those built-in, are designed primarily to read reflected light. It takes the variety of brightnesses and colours it sees and scrambles them to make an average. The resultant information is given as an aperture/shutter speed combination. The assumption is that somewhere in that conglomeration of tones, your main subject is in the middle. If that is so, all is well. And, for 99 per cent of the time, it works out right. For that other 1 per cent things can go horribly wrong.

Suppose your average portrait reading suggested 1/125th sec. at f8. If a very white background is positioned for a change, it will reflect so much light that we might get 1/125th

Two typical meter foolers. The first will catch the bright skylight and under-expose the subject; the second will be driven to over-exposure by permitting the dark background to undervalue the general exposure required. Measure the subject only for correct values.

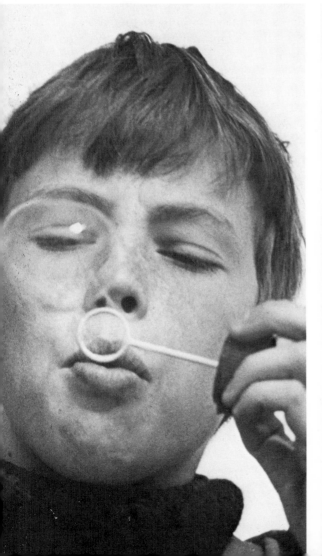
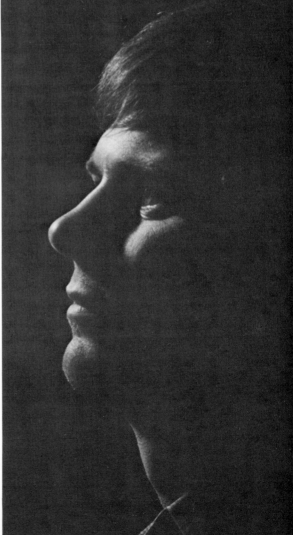

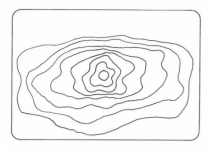

*The TTL 'centre-weighted' principle
Metering chart*

sec. at f16 – two stops less. The actual light on the subject has not changed, so it will be under-exposed by two stops. Exchange that for a black background, and the reading might be 1/125th sec. at f4 – two stops more. This time, the subject will be over-exposed.

You can overcome this problem of the meter giving false averages by taking the meter right up to the subject. Then, during the reading, the offending tones will not be able to influence the meter. But then we are faced with another problem. A meter will even 'average' a single tone. White, black or indifferent, it will fight gamely to make it an average middle grey. Check the grey scale and visualise how snow would look as a middle grey, or your friend's face, or a black cat. Not a pretty sight.

Problem shooting

There are three ways of overcoming this. You can, first of all, take a substitute reading of a mid-toned object, such as the back of your hand. As long as it is held in the same light as the subject, tones in the scene will fall into their correct places on the grey scale.

Secondly, you can use a 18 per cent reflectance Grey Card as a substitute. Kodak make one especially. This is precisely the grey the meter likes but it will only work effectively if it too, is held in the same light as the subject.

Falling light

Meters such as the Weston Euromaster can be used in the reflected mode or, with the addition of a translucent cone (illustrated), is turned into an incident meter.

Finally, you can take an incident light reading. When you measure the light falling on the subject, the meter is pointed towards the camera, and it cannot be affected by predominant tones in the picture area. In order to prevent it from reading the new scene behind the camera, the cell must be covered with a transluscent disc or, preferably, a dome. This is read by the cell as middle grey.

Using a camera in this way is cumbersome and a separate meter is much more practical.

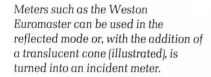

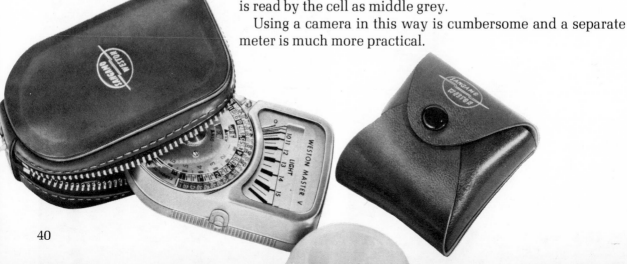

Soligor spot meter

Spot metering

Another meter category which seems to stand on its own is the spot meter. However, it does read reflected light but reads only a tiny portion of the subject rather than the 30-45° normally seen by a standard meter. The spot's coverage of around 1° makes it possible to read a small area of a distant subject but it does have the same problems as an ordinary meter, and the measurements have to be interpreted carefully.

To a certain extent, TTL metering through a telephoto lens is a sort of spot meter. Indeed, some have a switch-over 'spot' mode, or are centre weighted (paying more attention to the centre of the frame: see diagram, p. 40). But, good as they are, none of them read the narrow angle of the true spot meter.

It can be seen then, that a meter cannot always be taken on trust. Some brain power on your part is necessary too. But, as long as you tackle metering carefully, applying the methods suggested on the metering chart (see below), you will find that it is the only way of getting accurate exposures.

Subject	Reflected light method	Incident light method
Portrait	Measure the face only, excluding everything else	Standard reading from subject's position
Small or distant subject surrounded by contrasting tone, e.g. boat on bright water	Meter a substitute of similar tone, or a Grey Card, held in same light as subject	Standard reading in same light as subject
Landscape	Incline meter downwards to exclude sky	Standard reading
Subject in difficult light to camera	Meter close to the subject, in the same light	Standard reading
To increase shadow detail in general subject	Standard reading and open aperture by one stop	Standard reading and open aperture by one stop
To increase highlight detail in general subject	As above, but close down one stop	As above, but close down one stop
Light behind subject	Direct reading from subject, plus one wider stop for detail	Standard reading plus one wider stop
	Direct reading from light for silhouette	Point bare cell at light
Light too dim for general reading	Measure a white card and close down 4 stops	Use as reflected light meter with white card

4
Lighting principles

A statement was made earlier that a picture cannot be made without light. But, light by itself is not enough for a picture. Certainly, light enables us to see the subject, but we want to get an idea of its form, its dimensions. That is where shadows come in.

Let us go back a bit and establish a goal.

A picture is flat. It is, after all, only a piece of paper or film. But we want the images to look real and appear to have depth. Note how shadows do that. When they are seen in relation to highlights, they determine the shape. Angular shapes are clearly defined by the abrupt change from light to shadow; spherical ones have a much more graceful change with light gradually flowing into shadow. Other, more irregular shapes demonstrate their distinctive forms by combinations of both.

While light permits the subject to be seen, shadows reveal form and add to the sense of depth.

So, the simple rule is, light illuminates, and shadows reveal form. If we are to convey an impression of realism in our pictures, shadows are vital.

The shape of this building is distinctive because of the sharp angular shadows.

Seeing shadows

The artistic eye is one that has a clear vision of the effects of light and shade. This means re-focusing our impression of the subject and seeing it as a collection of interesting shapes revealed by a subtle blend of highlights and shadows. The actual nature of the subject is incidental.

Find a suitable object and try it. After you have observed the effects, move around it slowly. See how its appearance alters as light strikes it from different directions. Then, if it is movable, turn its most interesting 'face' around with you to see how the alterations of light/shadow relationship modifies it.

Take pictures as you go and make notes of the lighting angle for each shot. This will give you a visual record of lighting and a teaching chart all in one.

Natural lighting

We are accustomed to seeing things illuminated from above and to one side – 45° in each direction. That is how the sun does it. The subject looks good because the shadows present just the right impression of roundness – called modelling.

Try a lighting experiment on a friend. Use the mid-morning or mid-afternoon sun and position him so the light is falling on him in the ideal way described above. You will see how strong the appearance of depth is, of how the facial and bodily features are finely 'sculpted' by the shadows. Take a picture and draw a relevant lighting chart.

Next, move the subject around 45°, face him, and shoot again. Draw a chart, and move the subject another 45°. Repeat the process until you have turned full circle.

Finally, do the whole thing over at mid-day and late evening, when the sun is low.

Get that lot developed and printed and line them up in order, in three rows. Study them carefully and pick out those which have worked – where the lighting/shadow arrangement is flattering and form-revealing. When you then compare these pictures with your lighting charts, you will learn more about lighting than by reading thousands of words. In addition, you will have a ready-made lighting chart to work from.

Handling contrast

Knowing that your film can only cope with about seven stops of contrast, it is often prudent to check the subject's brightness ratio. Take readings of the deepest shadow in which you want detail and the brightest highlight, and count the number of stops in between – including the two measured. Where the subject is a face, for instance, seven stops is too much. Two is more like it (4:1 ratio) or, for colour, it should only be one (2:1 ratio).

If the ratios are too high, you can do something about it on some subjects. Remember, light reflects from bright surfaces. So, if you hold up a light card, cloth or paper, near and facing the shadow side, light will be reflected back in to brighten the shadows. Thus, the brightness ratio is lessened.

The brightness ratio can be reduced by the use of a reflector. In the right-hand picture the book has brightened the face to bring the ratio between the face and the background much closer.

If the light source is bright, use a matt-surfaced reflector. In a diffused light – such as a clouded-over sun, or under trees – then you can use something like tin foil or a mirror. Whatever you use, make sure it is not tinted if you are shooting in colour. It will reflect its own hue and you end up with colour shadows.

Light and distance

When you are taking pictures indoors by window light, or using a flash gun, photoflood, or ordinary household bulb, you have what is called a 'point light source'. Therefore, you will come up against the principle called the Inverse Square Law. This states that the intensity of the illumination falling on a surface is inversely proportional to the square of the distance separating them. In other words, if the lighting distance is doubled, the amount of illumination the subject receives is reduced by a quarter . . . and so on. As far as the sun is concerned, this does not apply. You would have to go some way off into space to explore the principle.

However, intensity is not the only change. Contrast is modified too. As you move a subject closer to a point light source, the contrast increases. You can test this yourself. Pose a friend close to the window, make a contrast check, and take a picture. Next move him further back into the room, and repeat the exposure procedure. You will see the difference clearly, and if you want to take a picture close to a window, you will have to use a reflector.

Shadows, then, are the key to the production of that vital impression of depth on flat paper. Certainly, the light is important, for without it we cannot take the picture. But that same shot is useless if there are no shadows, or if they are badly placed.

Work on it.

Filters for black and white

At times is is necessary to modify or adapt the content of light reaching the film. This is achieved by using a filter.

Thus, use of a filter in front of the lens alters the appearance of the colour of an object, or the scene as a whole. Therefore, the colours themselves on colour film, or the tones on black and white film, are shifted. This is able to happen because films of every type in general use are sensitive to all colours.

For instance, if you are shooting colour at high altitudes, or near the sea, the shadows appear to be blue in the finished pictures. This is because of the excess of ultra violet light. A UV filter stops that part of the spectrum entering the lens, and proper colour depth is restored.

Black and white films are just as sensitive. UV light has to be countered when using them too. While, of course, the effect is not seen as blue, there is a definite fall-off in detail and tone saturation. Objects in the distance are buried wholly or partially in a blanket of haze. A UV filter might help to cut through it but it is not as effective as a number of others available for monochrome work. In fact, most filters specifically designed for use with black and white photography reduce the effects of UV and haze.

The question might be asked, 'Other than cutting through haze, why use a filter at all? Can there be any legitimate uses when all you have to deal with are shades of grey?'

The answer to all that is 'yes'. Earlier we learned that the black and white film sees in brightnesses. To it, the objects it sees are not really coloured, but a degree of reflective brightness. Although everybody with normal eyesight sees the colours in objects, they also respond to the brightnesses. The eye knows, for instance, that a daffodil is brighter than fir trees. On monochrome film you expect the daffodil to be a lighter grey than the fir trees.

However, the panchromatic (sensitive to all colours) black and white film does not always respond to brightnesses in the same way as does the eye. For instance, it over-reacts to the sky, making it too dark on the negative and thus too light on the print. It tends to do that to red too, and yet under-values yellows and greens. In fact, the lightened red and darkened green come very close together in value on a monochrome emulsion. They both really reflect about the same amount of light. If you photographed a red fire engine standing on green grass, the two would tend to merge.

To correct these problems, you can press a filter into service. All it is really is a sheet of coloured glass in a holder which screws or clips onto the front of your lens. Its purpose is to lighten or darken specific tones and to achieve this filters are available in a variety of colours and strengths.

There is nothing mystical about using filters. To select the correct one for any given task you simply remember this rule:

> A filter for black and white allows to pass inhindered reflected light from objects of its own colour and reduces the amount reaching the film of other colours.

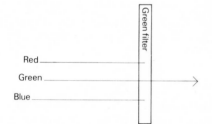

Let us use the three primary colours for our examples. A green filter allows all the green light to pass – that is reflections from green objects, and object hues which have green in them. Conversely, it will prevent a great percentage of both red and blue light (and hues which contain them) from teaching the emulsion. The nett result of all this is that greens will be lighter and reds and blues darker.

So, our fire engine and grass example mentioned above can be saved. The green filter separates the tones by making the grass lighter and the fire engine darker. Fit a red filter instead and, according to the rule of filters, you will get the opposite – dark grass and a light fire engine. In either case, the tones are pulled away from each other and the subject is much more clear in the final picture.

Of course, we do not always have only primary colours to deal with. Often the colours are complementary, or even mixes of many. Take yellow, for instance, a complementary colour. There is no need to panic. It still functions the same as all other filters. Yellow filters lighten their own colour and hues containing them (in some greens and reds, for example) and darkens other colours. Among those it darkens is its very own primary colour – blue. Therefore it has a useful function in that it darkens skies and prevents them from coming out too light in the final print.

A question of degree

The amount of alteration or re-balancing of light can be controlled. You merely have to select a filter of the right depth or strength.

Fundamentally, you can divide filters for black and white into two parts – correcting and contrast. There are no prizes for guessing that the first category are merely for correcting the tonal discrepancies you can expect in a scene. Likewise, it is fairly clear that the second category of filters are used to exaggerate those tone shifts.

In many cases, you have only the deepness of the colour of the filter to tell you which is which. For example, light and medium yellow filters are in the first unit, while deep yellow is in the second. A similar situation exists with greens, but there are others which are only found in one category or the other.

Most filters in the range for black and white work cut through atmospheric haze. However, do not always use one as a matter of course. Sometimes the atmosphere can be used as part of the composition.

The list looks something like this:

Correcting	Contrasting
Light yellow	
Medium yellow	Deep yellow
	Orange
Yellow-green	
Light green	
Medium green	Dark green
	Blue
	Red
	Deep red

Light loss

Filters alter the tonal values by absorbing some of the light. This means that some of the general intensity of light is reduced. Not as much light reaches the emulsion at a given exposure setting as would if there was no filter in place. You then have to adjust the exposure when using filters in order to compensate. If you do not, your pictures will be consistently under-exposed.

Fortunately, you can find out how much light is stopped by any given filter simply by reading the instructions, the filter box, and/or the rim of the filter itself. There you will find a figure which may look like this: 2X, or 7X, or some other number.

This figure is known as the 'filter factor'. It tells you how much extra exposure to give after you have taken a general reading without it. 2X means one stop extra exposure. You must open the aperture by an extra stop, after a reading, or slow down the shutter speed by one stop. By this reckoning then, 4X indicates an extra two stops exposure is required, and 7X suggests an extra $3\frac{1}{2}$ stops are needed, and so on.

Should you be the proud possessor of a single lens reflex camera with through-the-lens metering, have a care. Metering through the filter does not automatically compensate for the filter factor.

Sadly, TTL meters are of the Cds type and this type of cell does not respond to colours in the same way as does the film, or the eye. In general, the TTL meter undervalues the factor present in coloured light and will consistently under-expose your pictures. You have no choice but to take a reading without the filter first, then fit it, and then adjust for the filter factor manually afterwards.

If you think all that is a bit too cumbersome, there are short-cuts. For instance, if the light is generally constant,

Colour harmony is achieved by positioning two colours which are close to each other on the colour wheel together on the print or slide. In this case the green and blue harmonise but there is a hint of contrast for impact with the brown roof edge.

Use blur to mix colours. The
out-of-focus blur achieved by
selective focusing provides an
interesting example of different stages
of fuzziness and colour mixing. Only
in the background do you find that
blur has caused colours to merge and
mix to provide quite different hues.

The filter factor can make a great deal of difference to the exposure. If you have not compensated properly for it, you begin to lose detail in the shadows. In shots like this one, they are vital. To have lost detail in these shadows would have ruined the picture altogether.

your first meter reading will probably be fine for every exposure thereafter. You do not need to meter the subject again but can alter the factor as you change filters without further reference.

The alternative is to use a separate meter. That way you can leave the filter where it is and meter away to your heart's content, simply adding for the filter after the reading.

Filters in practice

Let us return to green again. It is a good colour to start with since it is usually in abundance wherever you look.

We have already examined one useful feature – the separation of green from other colours which have the same tonal value on the black and white emulsion. However, perhaps a far more interesting use is to help to increase detail and subtlety of tone in large masses of green. For instance, when

49

A green filter, for instance, helps to separate the various shades of green found in shots containing much foliage.

you are faced with large expanses of green foliage, all different hues of green, a green filter separates them clearly. You will be able to see the different hues in the form of a variety of greys.

Now, consider red. A richly stained mahogany top clearly shows its grain pattern if a red filter is used. Without it you are likely to see no pattern in the picture at all.

Perhaps the most common use of filters for black and white photography is to 'bring out' the sky. As we have already shown, there is usually so much brightness from the sky that it burns into the emulsion to make a blank white on the print. Through almost any filter (blue is a noted exception), the brightness is reduced and the blue darkened to make the clouds stand out.

The starting point for this effect is medium yellow, or yellow-green. For more dramatic effects, choose an orange for a dark grey sky, or red for one which appears to be almost black. All of them also cut back the effects of UV and haze to sharpen up the tonal saturation and detail in the distance.

Watch out for the position of the sun when working on the sky, however. It does make a difference to how much effect the filter can have. You achieve the maximum effect when shooting away from the sun. The more you turn into it, the less the filter darkens the sky.

If you like taking pictures of people, try a green filter when shooting out of doors, or a blue if working under photofloods. Both darken the skin and make it look suntanned and healthy. Avoid using orange and red filters on people under any circumstances. They both pick up the pink in skin and cause the subject to look pasty-faced and ill.

A blue filter is useful out of doors for special effects. It emphasises haze and mist, for instance, for better mood pictures. It allows you to produce the maximum separation between objects in the foreground and the mist-laden background for a greater appearance of depth. It also reduces contrast in bright sunlight. Blue light scatters. So, a contrasty scene 'passed' through a blue filter has its highlights

A deep filter – such as an orange – darkens the sky and separates it from clouds or, as in this case, smoke trails.

scattered into the shadow areas, causing them to appear to be lighter.

For more complete details, refer to the chart below. Do not feel you have to own every filter to be an effective photographer. You can get by with one or two – say a medium yellow, or yellow-green, a medium green, and perhaps an orange. Then, as you have to tackle a special task, buy the appropriate filter and build up your collection that way.

Filter	Uses
Medium yellow, or yellow-green	Scenery – darkens sky and adjusts tonal values to be more like those seen by the eye
Green	Lightens and separates foliage and other greens. Gives a healthy look to human skin
Orange	For stronger 'yellow filter' effects, particularly useful on buildings for lightening stonework and producing stark contrasts against a dark sky. Increases contrast and cuts through atmospheric haze
Red	For dramatic effects. Makes sky almost black. Red objects – and those containing red – become almost white. Contrast increased
Blue	Healthy skin appearance under photofloods. Outside, causes sky to be blank white, and increases the effects of haze and mist. Reduces contrast by scattering highlights into deep shadows

Filters for colour

Colour film, you will recall, is constructed of several different layers of emulsion, each sensitive to a different colour. When the film is processed you see through this sandwich for a combined effect which either more or less corresponds to those in the subject in a transparency, or the complementary colours in a negative.

The end result then (transparency or print) gives a fair imitation of what the colour in the original scene looked like. At least, we are fooled into believing it looks natural and we will stay fooled as long as we do not compare it too closely with the scene we photographed.

Casting your mind back again, you no doubt remember that so-called white light is rarely white. Often it is bluish to a degree, or reddish, and all casts in between. As the colour temperature of light alters, so does the response of the colour film. It is balanced for a specific temperature. Shoot it in that light and, exposure and other errors excepted, you can expect perfect results. Since it is difficult to find the right colour temperature all the time you must be prepared for some variations in the colour balance of the negative or transparency.

A reddish light – say early morning or evening – affects the red-sensitive layers more than it should. These come on strong and provide an overall reddish cast. Likewise, a bluish light turns the picture blue; the fluorescent lights turn it greenish, and so on.

The main purpose of filters for use with colour film is to put these effects right. Like the filter for black and white, it alters the colour content of light reaching the film and re-adjusts the temperature somewhere back to where it should be.

For example, you have in your camera a daylight colour film which is happiest working under lighting at a temperature of 5,500°K. This means that, for most of the day, you can shoot pictures without too much worry. But, when you arrive at the end of the day and want to shoot some portraits during sunset, the faces are bathed in a colour temperature glow of only 4,500°K. That is much too low and your pictured faces will be much too red.

You then examine your range of filters to find one which raises the colour temperature of the light reaching the film by 1,000°K. Logically, since the light is too red, you must find a bluish filter to lift the light up a bit. Easy, isn't it? Well, almost.

Before moving on to specifics, it is of great value to use filters where you can on colour film, even if you are using colour negative film. It is said that you need not worry too much with negative film since you can re-balance the colours during printing. Then it is achieved with specially graded filters in the enlarger (see Chapter 4).

However, if you are doing the printing, you want to make the job as easy as possible. Things will be difficult enough in the colour darkroom. So, use filters to produce a set of negatives all of which have more or less the same colour balance.

Colour compensation

Filters for colour can be loosely broken up into three groups. They are:

Colour compensating filters
Colour conversion filters
Creative filters

We have already glimpsed something of colour compensation work. But raising the colour temperature is only one job. Filters can be used to lower it as well. To achieve this, colour compensating filters are divided into two categories.

There are first the bluish filters already spoken about. These raise the colour temperature. Then there are the reddish filters which lower it. Each set of filters progresses from very pale to very dark. As the colour of the filter gets deeper, it raises or lowers the colour temperature to a progressively greater degree.

Now there are two important things about colour compensating filters. First, if you try to get every one, you will spend a small fortune and probably find that you never use them all. It makes much more sense to accustom yourself to the fact that some of your pictures will not be finely corrected and just have one or two well-placed filters from the complete range. Say, three bluish and three reddish, will do nicely and permit you to deal with a wide variety of colour temperature changes.

An 82B is a bluish filter which is popularly used for raising the temperature of evening light. An 81A is reddish and is used to lower the temperature on overcast days and give more natural looking colours. Choose an 80C (sometimes given a more convenient title of FL) for converting fluorescent lighting for use on daylight film.

The other point about raising and lowering temperatures is that the effects can be confusing. For instance, if your picture has an overall bluish appearance it is because the colour temperature was too high. A good example is when you have been shooting with electronic flash. However, confusingly, the appearance of the slide is said to be 'cool'.

It is so easy to get the cast appearance and the actual effects of the colour temperature mixed up. To repeat: bluish casts indicate a shooting colour temperature too high for the film, but the emotional value of the cast is cool. Likewise, reddish casts are caused by a temperature too low for the film, but they are said to be emotionally warm.

We will explore this issue in a later chapter. However, it is useful to have a sneak preview of this confusing problem at this stage.

Colour converters

This is perhaps a false category because colour conversion filters are found at the extreme ends of the colour compensating groups. A deep blue filter, usually given the number of 80B, will convert a daylight film for use in the much lower temperatured photoflood lighting.

For converting a film balanced for use in tungsten, or photoflood lighting, for daylight photography, you would use a deep red, or 85B, filter.

Indoor light differs from sunlight in colour content and can affect the performance of the film – particularly colour. If you use a daylight film, you have to shoot through a conversion filter.

In day-to-day photography, the latter method makes more sense than the former, if you are likely to be working both indoors and out on the same film. This is because of the filter factor. At the deep end of the filter scale they stop a lot of light, but the 80B is the worse of the two. If you use a film of – say – 100ASA and shoot through an 80B filter, up to two whole stops compensation would be required. This means that your film would no longer be 100ASA but effectively 25ASA.

On the other hand, an 85B filter only stops half a stop's worth of light. Therefore, your tungsten film, instead of being 100ASA would be about 80ASA.

Creative filters

The third group of filters extends the colour in film to almost way-out proportions. In some ways you can use any filter

55

creatively, but those especially designed to effect unusual results are the kind we will deal with now. In fact, there are so many that space does not permit listing and detailing them all. If you really want full information, you need only pick up one of the special booklets by Hoya, Ambico, or Cokin from any photographic dealer's. They are quite inexpensive.

Among those creative filters produced are single toned colours. These turn colour film into a sepia toned picture, or tobacco coloured, or blue, pink, and so on. Alternatively, you might choose a graduated filter, with one half coloured and the other half clear. These are great for darkening and colouring the sky whilst permitting the foreground to retain its natural colours. Some filters are dual and triple colours, which can be divided in half (two different colours), or in triangles (three different colours), or as a single colour with a clear or different coloured spot in the centre.

Daylight pictures with colour film are mostly straightforward but around the sea or at high altitudes there can be an excess of ultra-violet light. To counteract it, you have to employ a UV filter or a Skylight. The latter warms the scene as well as reducing the UV light.

Creative use of these filters is only bounded by your imagination.

Within this category there are some filters which can be used with equal effectiveness for colour or black and white film. There we find the UV filter and the Skylight for reducing haze. The latter one warms up the scene in colour as well.

Another is the polarising filter. This is a very popular one and is used for one of three purposes:

1. To eliminate or reduce reflections on shiny surfaces.
2. To reduce atmospheric haze.
3. To darken skies without altering any other colours or tones.

Light, when it strikes a surface, is reflected in all directions unless that surface is glossy. Then the reflection tends to be directional, that is to say, all in one direction. Such a reflection is called specular and is said to be polarised.

A polarising filter is able to stop these direct rays from reaching the film and show what the surface is really like, or what is below it. So, you can cut out the glare on highly polished wood, see through shop windows clearly with no glass reflections interfering, see below water for the same reasons, and reveal eyes behind spectacles.

However, it must not be overdone. It is possible to destroy the appearance of a shiny surface if you polarise too much and make it disappear. That way it looks unreal. A wet street no longer looks wet; a pool suddenly looks as though it has no water at all in it because all you can see is the bottom, and so on. Try to leave some reflection there to make things look more real.

Cutting through reflections in this way is how a polariser deals with atmospheric haze. All haze is, in reality, is light reflecting from tiny droplets of water in the air. The filter simply reduces the reflections and makes the distant scenery appear to be more saturated in colour or tone.

Whether on haze, or any other shiny surface, polarisers work best when the light strikes at an angle of 30°-35°. But when darkening the sky, it functions at maximum when the

To reduce or eliminate flare spots on water, you need a polarising filter. However, it can be overdone. If you polarise the light too much you can make all appearance of water present disappear.

sun is 90° to the angle of shooting. As you move the camera away from that angle, in any direction, so the darkening effect decreases. Indeed, the area is so limited that, on a wide angle lens, the polarisation effect can be quite different at the centre of the frame from at the edges.

One advantage with using a polarising filter to darken the sky is that it help you to show shadow detail. While this filter actually increases contrast, its action decreases the difference in the brightnesses of the sky and foreground. The brighter sky is brought lower down the scale, closer to the darker foreground, and you can then increase your exposure slightly to make sure of shadow detail in the subject.

Like all other filters, a polariser has a filter factor. However, because the polarisation effect is variable – it is changed by rotating the filter in the amount – the factor alters too. It generally ranges from about $2\frac{1}{2}X$ to $4X$.

Inasmuch as a polarising filter is not coloured, it can be used in conjunction with any other filter – for black and white and colour photography. However, you are then faced with two filter factors. This time, the problem is worsened because you do not simply add them, you must multiply them!

Filter	Effect
UV	Reduces blueness in shadows at high altitudes or close to sea. Cuts through atmospheric haze
Skylight	All the effects of the UV filter, plus it warms the scene slightly
Polariser	Darkens blue sky, cuts through haze. Eliminates or reduces reflections (achieves similar effects with monochrome film)
81A	'Warms up' dull day pictures
82B	'Cools down' sunsets or early morning pictures
80C (FL)	For eliminating the green cast in pictures taken in fluorescent lighting
80B	To convert a daylight film for use in photoflood lighting
85B	Converts a film balanced for tungsten light for use in daylight

Other creative filters which can be used for monochrome or colour are cross screen (for turning pin-points of light into stars); prisms (for producing multiple subjects from a single one on the same frame); split field (for making an ultra close up and a distant image at the same time on the same frame); fog filters (for softening the image); and so on.

In conclusion, the important thing about filters is that they must be chosen and used with care. Remember, you are putting more glass in front of your optically perfect lens. If the filter is not up to scratch, it will drag the optical performance of your lens down to its level. Always buy the very best you can afford. Finally, when using them, do not overdo it. Every colour picture you take turned sepia or blue becomes a bore after a while. Learn to have patience and use such filters only when you think the subject will benefit by it. Other than that, make filtering light a rewarding and creative experience.

A starburst filter coupled with flare produces some interesting effects.

Chapter Two The Picture

1

Realism and the photograph

How much like real life is a photograph? A photographer will go to extraordinary lengths to inject a sense of realism into his work because he wants to record or say something about life.

We have started on this road already with light and shadow to suggest an impression of depth which is not really there. But when it comes to actual realism, the pictures suffer one or two set-backs.

To begin with, the camera is capable of recording images which can be seen in no other way. It 'freezes' a tiny portion of fast continuous movement or, with the aid of a long, long exposure, reveals objects when it is too dark for us to see. In this sense, then, it is *more* than real.

It is the frame surrounding the image in the viewfinder which makes a picture *less* than real. The view seen with your naked eye is boundless. It knows no borders. When it sees something vast, the eye unconsciously darts about, drinking in the view in a series of angles which are absorbed by the brain as one. No camera can do that. It takes only a portion of that breathtaking scene and ushers it into the confines of four borders. This is why pictures of scenery are

often so disappointing. That incredible view suddenly becomes flat and insignificant.

Naturally, this is something you can fight. If you take the very disadvantages and turn them around to work for you, the picture will be advanced towards realism in a different way.

Practical viewfinding

Use the viewfinder border consciously. When you spot something worth committing to film, spend some time studying it through your viewfinder. Forget what you saw before and now begin to make the view look good in those four borders. And, before you shoot, check:

1. That nothing is projecting awkwardly through the corners and edges of the frame to take the eye away from the central image
2. That the horizon is level
3. That the background is not so distracting that it competes with the subject

Now press the button.

The golden rule

The most difficult task confronting you when taking a photograph is deciding what to leave out. No cameraman has any problems over his decisions about what to include. Indeed, many cram in everything in sight. The resultant picture is much too busy and of no interest to anyone.

A good picture is simple. You pick a subject and concentrate on that. Anything which does not contribute must be cut out. If something else in the scene vies for attention, it deserves another picture all to itself.

This makes photography a process of selection. We pick and choose those things which interest us and use the frame to isolate it in a square or oblong chunk of reality. But even that is too loose a description. Having decided where to point the camera, the frame is then used ruthlessly to select from and simplify the selection. The object of this exercise is to make a picture which has instant appeal – or impact. It has to tell whatever story it is supposed to tell in the most direct manner possible. Where the subject of the picture is in doubt, it has failed.

Simplicity must be your watchword.

Note how the second cropping has simplified the picture and united the important figures in it. The decimation of the head on the right has emphasised the ear and made it appear as though he was trying to overhear.

Seeing the subject

Such a picture is made in the viewfinder. Once you press the button, it is too late. Study the subject and try to find its most basic elements. Move around to find a shooting angle which shows them off the clearest with line, form, shape, and light and shadow.

To help you decide how much of the subject and/or the surrounding area to leave in, ask yourself about it. What does it contribute to the subject and enhance it? Can the subject stand without it? Would the subject be better served if only a part of it were photographed, rather than the whole? In time, your eye and brain will do all this work without conscious interrogation. For the moment, however, give yourself a thorough going-over in order to hone a keen edge on your photographic vision.

You have three 'mechanical' aids to help you select and simplify:

1. *Camera-to-subject distance*
   The simplest form. As you move back and forth, you alter the amount 'seen' by the viewfinder.
2. *Change of focal length*
   Through a special viewfinder on a rangefinder camera, or the lens itself of an SLR, you can choose a focal length which eliminates all unwanted detail. This is where a zoom lens comes into its own. You can alter the focal length on camera (SLR) and watch the changing effect of the composition all the time. There is no break while you have to change lenses. Also, you can choose any focal length you like. Your final decision may be 119mm. Try finding a fixed focal length of that size!

3. *Selective enlarging or copying*
This really should be kept as a tidying-up process only. Too great enlargements or selective copies only serves to deteriorate the image, and it is best to fill the frame to simplify the image as much as you can when shooting. Nevertheless it is there as a back-up.

Picture depth

Much has been said in this section about the importance of realism in a picture. Nothing knocks realism in the head more than a lack of depth. So, because the image is two-dimensional, it is necessary to resort to trickery to create the desired impression.

The most prominent method is depth of field. It will play some sort of role in every photograph you take whether or not you are conscious of it. When you focus, sharpness does not fall off immediately in front of and behind the subject. It is gradual, creating a band of sharpness each side of the optically sharp plane.

What happens is this: points on the optically sharp plane register on the negative as points; but those each side of that plane begin to go fuzzy and register as blurred circles. The further they are from the focus point, the larger and more blurred they get. However, human vision confuses these early blurred circles with dots because they are so small. And as long as they remain tiny enough to fool us, we think that area is actually sharp. The name for this phenomenon is very apt – 'circles of confusion'.

Depth of field can be seen in action here. The point of optical sharpness is the white-faced individual with the apple. Sharpness falls off slowly in front of and behind him to indicate the limits of acceptable sharpness. With the wide aperture and long focal length lens used here, depth of field is minimal.

Once the dots pass the size of 1/50th in., we are no longer confused. From that stage on, the image gets progressively unsharp. The apparent in-focus area is known as the depth of field.

Depth control

Depth of field can be extended or shrunk at will, in four different ways:

1. *Aperture control*
A wide aperture shrinks depth of field, a small one stretches it.
2. *Camera/subject distance*
Photograph close to the subject and, whatever the aperture, the depth of field is narrow. Move further away and it gets progressively deeper.

3. *Focal length*

Telephoto lenses progressively shrink depth of field the longer they get, whereas wide angles increase it.

4. *Enlargement/projection*

As you enlarge the image, the little circles grow bigger too. When they pass the 1/50th in. mark, the image appears to be out of focus because of the shrinking of the depth of field.

In method 4, to make sure you have as much depth of field as you need, you must provide a large enough buffer during the taking stage. For the other three, control is managed in two ways.

First, a depth of field scale is engraved on every lens barrel. The centre mark is, in fact, the point against which you focus. Repeated on both sides are the aperture settings, starting at the widest and extending out to the smallest.

You simply focus on a subject and then read off the footages adjacent to the two marks which correspond with the aperture you are using, on the depth of field scale. With a 52mm lens focused on 10ft, for example, and with f11, it shows that everything from $7\frac{1}{2}$ ft to 15 ft will be acceptably sharp.

The second method applies only to SLRs. You can see how much depth of field you have just by closing down the aperture to the stop you intend to use. If your camera does not have a depth of field preview button, press the shutter release part way down.

Playing with sharpness

With a narrow depth of field you can select a portion of the image and simplify it by throwing everything else out of focus. It will then stand out as an apparent third dimension from the unsharp areas. This narrow band of sharpness can be used to isolate the foreground, middle ground, or background and separate it so that the eye is immediately drawn towards it.

However, selective focusing is not the only means of creating an impression of depth. Where the picture is in focus throughout, the eye follows sharp, interesting objects from the foreground, through the middle to infinity. The direction of travel makes the viewer feel he is looking 'into' the scene. In attempting this effect, a small aperture and a wide angle lens may not be enough. You may have to resort to a depth of field manipulation called the 'hyperfocal distance' (see photograph below).

Ordinarily, depth of field extends to one-third in front of the optically sharp plane, and two-thirds behind. As that area

The hyperfocal distance technique permits widely spaced objects to be brought into focus at the same time. In this case, a wide angle lens has been used to increase the depth.

Shifting depth of field in relation to the subject

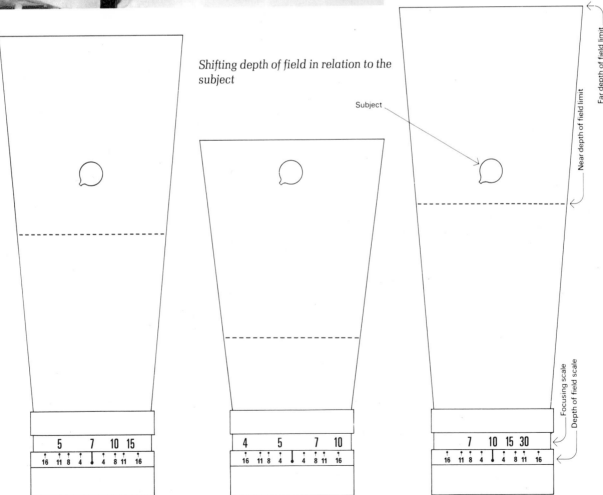

Subject

Far depth of field limit

Near depth of field limit

Focusing scale

Depth of field scale

is all acceptably sharp, it does not really matter where the subject is within it. So, if you shift focus slightly, you can position the subject at the front or rear edge of the sharp area for changes of emphasis.

But the real hyperfocal bonus occurs when you are focused on infinity. Everything beyond the infinity mark is in focus anyway, and that means two-thirds of the depth of field is wasted. So, by shifting focus slightly again, we can place 'infinity' on the rear edge of the depth of field and get the extra bonus of focus, in front.

Move infinity from the centre point on your depth of field scale to the mark corresponding to the aperture in use. Just by looking at the scale, you can see the difference. You have half as much sharpness again. A 52mm lens at f11 extends sharpness to 15ft, whereas it was 30ft before. Just about everything in the picture would be in focus.

Separating planes

This technique is most useful when incorporating a frame or foreground object. Many subjects lose impact in pictures because the impression of space is reduced. Something in the foreground – like a rock, fence, tree, building, or whatever – enables the viewer to assess the relationships of size. He compares this object with the background and 'sees' depth.

People can be used too, but they should be fitted in as naturally as possible. Rather than having them stare into the camera to create a conflicting image, pose them looking at the view, or strolling through the scene. The viewer will see the figures first, but then he will look to see what they are looking at – and see the view.

A frame differs slightly from a foreground object in that it serves to isolate the main subject as well as providing a foreground reference. Trees are commonly used. The sweeping curves from the roots, up the trunk, to the branches contain the background image, stopping dominant lines from leading the eye out through the picture edge. In addition, the fact that it seems to stand forward suggests another plane within the picture.

Tonal depth

Tonal values are significant when using foreground objects or frames. People are prone to a rather interesting – and, where photography is concerned, useful – phenomenon. Dark tones appear to be lying on more forward planes than light ones. Likewise, dark and well-saturated colours seem to stand in front of lighter, weaker ones. Therefore, if the foreground object or frame is dark – perhaps even a silhouette – it is given a greater 'lifting' boost, appearing to stand well forward of the lighter background.

Haze, mist and fog produce similar effects. Water droplets, dirt and dust hang in the air and reduce the sharpness and clarity of distant subjects. A telephoto lens seems to exaggerate it but that is because it is usually used to photograph distant objects. A shorter lens includes much more foreground where the haze is not as noticeable. Therefore it is better saturated in tone or colour and stands out.

Mist, fog and smoke create even more startling effects. In these cases, the background can disappear completely, leaving not only startling separation, but also a strong sense of mystery.

Perspective

A natural means of giving the illusion of depth to a picture is with perspective. You know that same-size objects appear to diminish in size as they get further from the eye. It enables you to form some judgement about distance. As this effect is recognised in real life, it is accepted in a photograph and interpreted as depth.

To make full use of perspective, we have to become aware of dominant lines. Examine any subject long enough and you will eventually see them. Take a street scene, for example.

If you stand at the kerb side, looking down the street, the first dominant line is the kerb, running straight down the

Both types of perspective are shown in this picture. Linear perspective is evident in the diminishing size of the fence posts, and the converging verticals. Atmospheric perspective is shown by the gradual fall-off of clarity as the scene disappears into the mist.

middle. To your left you find the line where the pavement meets the building or wall. Then there are the tops of the buildings, door and window tops and bottoms – all forming lines zooming off into the distance. On the right, there are even more.

Although these lines are actually parallel, they appear to converge. If uninterrupted, they would continue to converge until they met all together, at the horizon – the vanishing point. From time to time, you might see breaks in these lines, and new ones projecting off in different directions to form vanishing points elsewhere on other parts of the horizon. However, it is not difficult to sort out these secondary lines and recognise those which are dominant.

Not all lines are as obvious as this. Many are obscure and require some visual study before they become evident. Once they have been discerned, however, you need only to adjust your viewpoint to be able to usher them into a strong depth-giving composition.

Picture space

Having dealt with space longitudinally, so to speak, we must now look at it laterally – across the image plane. For how you position objects within the four picture borders is of vital importance.

What you have to work with is an empty space surrounded by a frame. But while this space might be empty, it is not static. There are many hidden forces at work. They come from the border and act like magnets, attracting any object which comes within their influence. However, since they all have the same power, a centrally positioned object is acted upon equally by all sides and stands still. Indeed, it is so static, it runs the risk of being boring. Avoid it, unless you wish to convey a feeling of rest.

When a subject is placed off-centre, it comes under the influence of its nearest border. The 'pull' suggests movement and the subject immediately captures attention. The strong off-centre line is said to be one third of the way into the space. Psychologically, the right hand one is stronger, and movement is more commanding if the image appears to be travelling from left to right, moving into the picture. However, considerable interest is generated if the subject seems to be moving out of the picture. It is unexpected and commands attention.

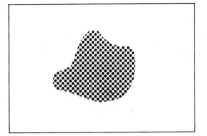

A subject placed centrally is at rest

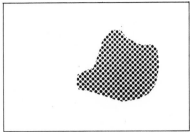

When that object is off-centre, a sense of movement is present

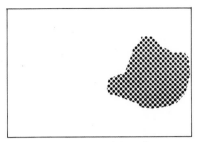

Close to the edge and that object is in conflict

The corner is the strongest of all and objects appear to be drawn through with great force

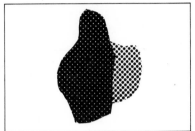

If you have more than one subject, make one dominant to avoid symmetry

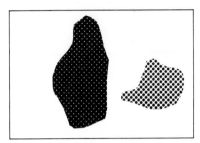

Proper balance is achieved with the larger object close to the centre, and the smaller one nearer the edge

Where the power is

Such an image is particularly powerful if it is close to the frame edge. The force is stronger there and it appears as though the subject will be drawn outside the picture altogether.

Right at the edge, however, conflict occurs. The feeling of movement out of the frame is strong, but the border is also a 'wall', ready to repel the oncoming object. It is an area of considerable influence, drawing immediate attention. If that object close to the edge is not important, it will draw the eye away from the main subject.

The most powerful influence is exerted by the corners where the forces of two edges meet. An object positioned close to a corner seems to be speeding out of the picture. Unless there are 'containing' factors of some sort, the eye will follow the projected trajectory right out through the corner. The picture is then lost. The greatest evidence of this is when dominant lines are permitted to run out through the corner – or, indeed, any edge. The eye soon finds them in the print and follows them right away from the centre of interest.

Multi-subjects

Often, you will have more than one subject at a time to deal with in a photograph. The important thing is to avoid

Objects close to the edge are in conflict. The ski jumper appears to be dragged forward by the frame edge and thus a strong feeling of movement is present. However, the border also represents a wall and conversely seems to be about to repel the oncoming figure. As a result the viewer is agitated lest the skier comes a cropper.

symmetry. That gives equal importance to them both and creates conflict. Make one dominant. Position it higher, or make it larger. If they are partially overlapped too, you will only have a single mass to position in the frame.

Handle overlapping with care. Remember, the flatness of the paper thrusts two widely separated objects together. All kinds of annoying and amusing situations result if you do not watch what is going on in the viewfinder. Poles grow out of heads, hands grow out of noses, and statue wings grow out of shoulders.

Balance and timing

At times, widely separated subjects will not come together. Provided one is dominating through size, it is still possible to create a pleasing image by using the balance principle of the fulcrum.

The large subject placed near the centre balances with the smaller one, placed closer to the edge (see diagram on p. 69). The latter cannot be too near the picture edge, mind you, or it will draw too much attention. The correct balance means that both subjects will receive their due attention and be accepted as a single, unified image.

Sometimes, one or other of these subjects is moving. The principle still applies. You must wait for it to get into the correct balance position before committing it to film. Therefore, there is another factor to take into account – time. If that means waiting for a car to arrive at a certain point – or even to come into view – in order to make the elements gel, so be it. If it means following a moving subject until it arrives at a point where all other background and foreground objects combine to balance the image correctly, you must do it.

To balance two moving subjects using the fulcrum method is a question of timing. You must wait until the subjects are in the right positions before you shoot. Remember, the picture is made before you press the shutter release.

Because a subject is moving, it will not necessarily make a good picture all by itself. Get everything together.

However, the nature and tone of subjects have a modifying influence. Loud colours and contrasting tones, no matter how small, will capture the eye. 'Small' people will too. Where they are counterbalancing a large inanimate subject, they command attention far out of proportion to their size. People, regardless of their tiny proportion, attract people.

Mood

Large areas of dark tones or warm colours (oranges, reds, etc.) have an effect on the overall mood of the picture. For instance, light clouds over a dark landscape suggest a happy, summery day. On the other hand, dark, ominous clouds overhead threaten and suggest foreboding.

Lines are emotional too. They carry the eye where you want it to be, helping it to scan the image and experience the total emotional value. Because the eye moves with lines, just as sure as if arrows were marked on them, it has added its own feeling of action. This can be very useful in action pictures. The trick is to stop the line taking the vision right out of the picture.

Dynamic lines – those which suggest movement the most strongly – are diagonal. These can suggest depth (as in perspective diagonals), or lie on the surface (as in the end view of a roof). Other surface or flat lines are verticals and horizontals. Therefore, if you oppose the flow of a dangerous line with another, the eye is checked and perhaps even redirected. Thus the upright corners of buildings on our street scene earlier, and side streets with their own new diagonals, check our vision flow along the street and cause us to stop

The flowing lines of the bird's wings, on down through its body to the head and beak, strongly suggest graceful movement.

and look. The image, then, is beginning to capture the interest.

Skilled use of lines means that you can pick a viewpoint which contains the eye by leading it continually back to the main subject. A foreground frame is a prime example. The eye might wander back and forth between background and frame, but it cannot escape. And, the more it lingers on, the greater the impact, and the longer the picture will be remembered.

Shape and line

The circular or oval frame suggested by the tree is a pleasing shape. But it need not only be supplied by a frame. If the position of the subject suggests a regular shape, then it has a similar emotional influence.

A triangular shape, the right way up, spells stability and strength, while an inverted one gives the impression of uncertainty and imbalance. A square is static and uniform, while an upright oblong is majestic. If the oblong is horizontal, then, like the circle or oval, the impression is peacefulness and rest.

While the lines already mentioned mirror their shape counterparts, there are others. Curved, sinuous lines suggest depth, as well as a flowing movement. If those lines are jagged, like lightning, you have an impression of frenetic activity. Uprights, curved gently at one end, 'ripple' as does corn swaying in the breeze; but if that line is curved into a 'C', or a full circle, the eye follows it around and around and is contained. However, an unbroken circle makes the composition boring because eye travel is unrelieved. And you certainly don't want that. The name of the photographic game is to stimulate and excite.

Rhythm, pattern, and texture

Photographic vision is something more than just spotting subjects such as a nice building or a pretty girl. It means looking deeper than that. Instead, you strive to recognise the value of sometimes the most unlikely objects. Here, the subject itself is not important – rather are the special relationships between light and shade; the sweep of the lines; the contours of form; the values of shape.

Therefore, just about anything is suitable as a subject for a photograph. It need not be breathtaking, or even pretty; indeed, it may be an ordinary, everyday subject which is not

You can control the appearance of a colour by altering the exposure. A one stop shift makes a considerable difference and evokes a completely different feeling. The darker of these two pictures of a rose was given the correct exposure. The lighter one was over-exposed by one stop. If it had been negative film, the same effect could have been produced by under-exposing.

Under the evening sun you will see the warm effect of reddish light. It can be quite pleasing – and effective for producing three-dimensional effects – provided you do not wait until the sun is too low.

Cool colours appear around water, particularly in and around noon. However, any picture which is dominantly blue can be said to be cool.

even seen as a possible picture by anyone else but you. That is why you will see pictures of such things as shapes in a stone wall, a pattern of shadows on the ground, or a doorknob and a keyhole. None of these things are intrinsically exciting subjects, but when the photographer sees them and puts them on film creatively he has made a picture of something which did not really exist before.

Naturally, not every shot you take must be of subjects as abstract as these to be a success. In fact, even in quite standard subjects you may find visual ideas which help you to find a way of taking a personal and unique photograph – even though it has been photographed a million times in the past.

There are three basic elements of picture composition which set you on the road towards achieving this: rhythm, pattern, and texture. These three are vital parts of the complete image. However, they are not always all used at once. You can employ just one, two, or all three to make your picture. Then again, sometimes, the power of the subject makes them secondary; at others they are the picture.

Rhythm

Rhythm provides a feeling of movement in an otherwise static picture. As its name suggests, it is the use of a repeated theme, object, shape, or whatever. When you get it right, it can be as emotional to the person seeing the picture as when he hears the repetitious rhythms in a symphony, or a pop song. A repeated shape causes the eye to move across from one to the other and experience action.

You can do this in pictures which are normally still. Take a landscape, for instance. The inclusion of a row of fence posts, trees, a line of hills, etc., adds a feeling of movement to make the picture much more lively and interesting. The eye follows the shapes in the direction in which they diminish in size.

Putting rhythm in pictures is not easy. There are dangers here as there are with lines. The eye will be just as happy to follow its rhythmic passage out of the picture frame as it will to travel in any other direction. It is important to make sure your rhythms run towards the centre of interest in order to strengthen and unify the image.

You do not have to search for rhythmic shapes which are all identical. Indeed, they can be completely different. As long as they have a similar appearance – a sea swell coupled with rolling hills, for example – the visual experience will work. And this is where a photographer's eye is so important.

Rhythm is present in the repeated shapes of the canoes and the figures. The fact that they are one in front of the other encourages the feeling of forward movement and this is strengthened by the three oar positions: it might almost be an instructional diagram on how to use an oar. Yet, while they strongly 'pull' the image forward, they also provide the variety to prevent the picture becoming boring.

It is easy to see rhythm in identical subjects, and quite another to work unrelated ones into the picture in a meaningful and exciting way.

If you do use identical objects to achieve your rhythm, make sure there is some difference somewhere along the line. Too much similarity makes for a monotonous and mechanical picture. You need variety in spacing, size, shape, or tonal or colour value to enliven the composition and surprise the viewer. Do not go too far though. If the rhythm is too varied, it becomes obscure and the 'beat' is lost, just like – say – the rhythms in Chinese music might be lost to your ear. Variations are meant to be a slight, occasional change to the visual beat; there to add interest as the varied rhythms in a piece of music.

Pattern

Where rhythm lines or shapes cover a major part of, or the entire picture area, then you have pattern.

A pattern photograph is usually almost abstract. For instance, look at your wallpaper. The pattern there is solely to brighten up a plain surface. Without it, your walls would be dull. Another thing about it is that it does not require you to do anything. Your eye is not drawn to any particular spot and moves over the pattern freely because there is no centre of interest. As a result, pattern seems to be flat. Even if the objects which make up the pattern in a photograph are three-dimensional, it still appears to lie on the surface.

So, you might ask yourself, 'What is the use of pattern when we are trying to fool the world into believing a picture has depth?' Surprisingly, an occasional pattern photograph can be most exciting. To begin with, it shows and emphasises detail no-one might ever have noticed before. That is of interest. Moreover, the viewer can see the creation of a satisfying design and even order. People like order.

When you look for patterns, you find them in the most unlikely places. They appear in parts or rows of houses, trees, branches, lines of books, corn stubble, and so on. Find the patterns, isolate them in your pictures and they suddenly become visually exciting.

But, as with rhythm, geometry equals monotony. There has to be variety, or an accent, in the pattern to stimulate and keep interest. By seeking out and including a change in spacing, or a subtle alteration in shape, tone, or colour, you provide an attraction for the eye to keep coming back to. It is then prevented from wandering aimlessly around the picture – as it does with wallpaper – and eventually out of the frame altogether.

Sometimes, pattern is the only way you can make something interesting out of the subject you see. A mass of small detail is a good example. You can only turn it into an effective picture by emphasising a consistent or repeated feature (with occasional variations) that you have discovered in the chaos. At other times, you may create pattern for effect. When you use a telephoto, for instance, the 'squashed' together planes caused by the perspective of distance turn angular and flowing shapes into pattern-like arrangements.

Pattern is a most useful means of intensifying form and

The pattern created by the orderly rows of punts flattens out and contrasts sharply with the punt with figures. That one has depth. The two together strengthen each other.

depth. Remember how two or more dissimilar objects in contrast strengthens both by emphasising the features of each other. It happens too when a well-modelled landscape is framed by a silhouetted – and therefore flat – tree, or when a patterned wall or floor is contrasted with a human figure. The flatness of the pattern and the three-dimensionality of the landscape and figure are both emphasised.

If you make pattern too strong and allow it to dominate, however, it can destroy the appearance of depth in a three-dimensional subject. Shadows from a tree and its branches covering an object with depth will flatten it. The shadow/pattern dominates. Likewise, a heavily patterned background will appear to suck the subject in front right into it and make it a part of the overall pattern.

Texture

A pattern which covers and shows up the nature of the surface of the object is texture. It is usually emphasised when the light strikes the surface at an acute angle (side-lighting). The light picks out the bumps or projections, and casts shadows in the 'valleys' or depressions.

Now, texture is most valuable for making an otherwise uninteresting area catch the eye. But, more important, texture can fool the viewer into believing that he can feel the quality of the subject's surface if he reaches out and touches it. In other words, it adds a strong sense of realism.

The textural qualities of this leaf and the snow are emphasised by the cross lighting and each is strengthened by the presence of the other. Indeed, the 'feel' is so marked that the viewer is tempted to reach out and touch the surfaces of the subjects.

When you think about it, objects are recognised by their surfaces. Chrome is smooth; wood is rough; silk is sleek. If you can capture those qualities in your pictures visually, they can be instantly recognised and you have added that necessary reality.

Texture can also be used as a means of 'separating' subjects which may look alike in tone or colour and are next to or overlap each other. Where there is no texture visible, they merge and become a single visual unit. However, when two differing textures are placed close to each other, not only can you recognise them as two separate units but an emotional effect also occurs.

A rough texture next to a smooth one will appear to be rougher (and, because of the contrast effect, the smooth one smoother) and with the larger shadow pattern, it will seem to be darker. Since dark tones 'project' forward, the object it is describing is emphasised. If the smooth one is not to be overwhelmed, you must find a new viewpoint which makes use of natural perspective to increase its apparent size.

Remember, you can only show texture by cross-lighting. Flat, head-on lighting kills it. Generally speaking, diffused side-lighting is sufficient to reveal the quality of rough surfaces. A smoother texture, however, requires strongly directional illumination, such as a spot light, or the direct sun.

Colour composition

If photography is a language and you can speak it in black and white to share your emotions, you can express yourself in colour too. In certain circumstances, it is easier to produce interesting pictures in colour than it is in monochrome. Think about it. The biggest thing going for colour is that you can see the subject in colour instead of in shades of grey. You see life this way. That the picture's colours are not quite like the real thing is unimportant. That colours of some sort are there, is.

This does not necessarily mean that colour is any better than black and white. On the contrary, both have their place in the scheme of things. Both can be used to show a single image in different ways, revealing different moods. More than that, however, there are subjects which work best in black and white, and others which look better in colour. Neither would be at their best the other way round.

Naturally, the entire thing depends on your approach to using colour. It is so easy just to point your camera and shoot, knowing that the colours which are there are going to record.

But that is the negative way. All you are doing then is recording. You are not creating memorable colour pictures. There is much more to effective colour photography than that. You have to work at using colour; employ it as an important part of the image. In other words, you have to be a positive, active colour worker.

And yet, generally speaking, a photographer loaded up with colour film has to take the hues in a subject as he finds them. There are a few things he can do to adjust them. As we have already learned, he can, for instance, use filters to warm up or cool down colours; he can modify the exposure to intensify or de-saturate them; and so on. However, he does not have the freedom of the painter who can exercise absolute control by leaving out or adding whatever colours he likes.

Nevertheless, there is much a colour photographer can do to bend it to his will. The first step is to learn not to take colour for granted. Instead, learn to appreciate the relationships and reactions of colours with each other. This is vital to the colour photographer. There is no other way of making colour pictures say something. The two or more hues you put together physically, by choice of viewpoint, can make the world of difference, not only to the colours you have made neighbours, but also to the message you are endeavouring to promote through your picture.

The colour wheel

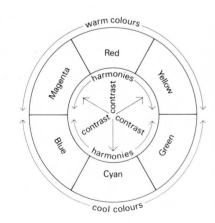

The key to this is to become throroughly familiar with the 'colour wheel'. The wheel is like a spectrum really, only the colours are neatly arranged in a circle. No account is taken of the colour temperatures except that the warm colours are arranged around the top half of the wheel, and the cool colours around the bottom. As you already know, warm hues have a more or less red base, and cool hues contain some blue. The arrangement of colours is also neat enough to make sure that the colours opposite each other are complementary. These then are said to be in contrast. So, yellow contrasts with blue. When placed next to each other in a picture – say, a yellow flower against the sky – they produce an image with impact. A similar situation exists with green and magenta, and red and cyan.

Now, here is a most important difference between colour and black and white. Contrast has an extra meaning in colour. In monochrome, light and dark makes the most important contrast. While this kind exists in colour too, it also finds meaning in a primary and its complementary in juxtaposition. This means that two soft and delicate colours which you would not even think of as being extreme – like light and dark – can be in contrast if they are complementary to each other.

Those colours which stand side by side on the wheel are said to be in harmony. You find harmonies in blues and greens; greens and yellows; yellows and oranges; oranges and reds. These work well together and produce pleasing images.

Just this brief introduction to the use of colour emphasises the need to approach colour photography throughtfully. You can also see that a cameraman is not so different from a painter in some ways. Both must 'see' the scene in the same way. Both must carefully recognise the colour values present and decide how best to use them.

Colours have feelings

We have already said that the reds, oranges and yellows in the colour wheel are visually warm, and the blues and greens are cool. Everyone experiences at least unconscious emotions about warm and cool colours. It is a natural reaction on our part. Think about it. Not only do cool colours make us feel cold, but they also appear to be more distant. Warmer colours, on the other hand, give us a warm feeling and, what is more, appear to be closer to the eye.

Nature has conditioned us to recognise these effects simply because atmosphere makes objects in the distance look cool (bluish). Distant colours also look less intense. Atmospheric haze does this by de-saturating the colours in the background and causing them to seem to be pastel shades or even, in extreme cases, washed out and insipid. The relative lack of haze between nearby objects and the camera allows the full strength of the colours to reach the camera. They are powerful and well-saturated.

To return to blue, it has another, deeper emotional value too. We get blue with cold, for instance, and, with it, un-happy. Thus, as the blue gets deeper and dominates in a picture, the feeling is one of melancholy.

At the other end of the spectrum scale, the warmer reds and oranges suggest sunshine, heat and comfort. However, in contrast, you also wave a red rag to a bull to get it angry. So reds also create feelings of anger, irritation, passion and even danger when there are plenty of them in a picture.

Other colours, too, express their own feelings. Some of them are personal but this list should help you to define some of the emotions evoked and make use of them in your colour pictures.

Warm colours

Red

Warm and relaxing when appearing in small doses. Also shows anger, aggressiveness, passion and danger. Just to make things difficult, when handled with care, red can also express love.

Orange

More or less as above but as it is a sort of diluted red it expresses the emotions with less intensity. Indeed, it is more positive in that it is more likely to be warm and relaxing than irritating or depicting danger. It can also show creativity and imagination.

Pink or magenta

This is a natural colour for showing purity and innocence. It can also express riches but if it is not used carefully it can create feelings of obstinacy.

Yellow

Suggests love on the one hand and deceit on the other. But its strength also implies riches and, to a certain extent, sturdiness because its colour can almost always be seen, even in very dim lighting.

Mauve

A colour of affection. Remember, it is the colour used by kings and queens. However, it is also used to suggest death. It can depict vanity as well as emotional uncertainty.

Cool colours

Blue

Distant but pleasing. As blue is the colour of the 'heavens' it expresses also knowledge and truth – even holiness. Blue is also said to depict loyalty and steadfastness. On the negative side, blue also expresses melancholy, the 'blues' and pessimism.

Green

This is the colour of the young. As in Spring, it suggests youth but, as youth is often not, it can also be very tranquil and restful. This is the opposite to blue in that it expresses optimism and that everything is normal and safe. A lot of green in a picture is easy on the eye – and the nerve endings.

Yellow-green

There are too many shades of green to detail here but this one in particular is a difficult one to handle. It is an upsetting colour, suggesting illness or sickness.

Neutral colours

Black

This is said to be no colour at all, but as it often appears in pictures, it should be treated as a colour. Where there is too much of it in a picture, the image shows despair, moodiness and all the other feelings expressed under the chapter dealing with black and white. While you use only a little, it shows strength or, at least, strengthens the image overall.

White

The problem with white is that it is fickle. It is always ready to pick up and show, as a weaker version, any of the nearby colours. Therefore, it is difficult to produce a true white on colour film. Where you can get it, though, it shows innocence and purity. It is also a clean colour with a special power of its own and can depict happiness and gaiety. Be sparing with it, however. As in real life, too much white in a picture is hard on the eye.

Brown

This is the colour of the earth and suggests a rugged strength, responsibility, and wisdom. It is also restful but if dominating in a picture it can be too dull and inactive.

White is a most difficult tone to get right on a colour emulsion. It tends to pick up and reflect other colours around it. Moreover, if there is too much of it, the eye finds it difficult to look at. Treat it with care, using it sparingly and in a way that effectively makes use of stark compositions.

Subtle colours, such as you expect in these flamingoes, are readily captured on colour film which has a hue very close to the original colour. However, since they are light colours they respond readily to exposure differences. Give too much and the colour turns out too deep; give too little and it is too light. There is very little latitude for exposure error with colour film.

Emotion is controlled by the amount of any colour which you include in the shot. Where it dominates and where it is intense, the emotion is very strong. However, you can 'dilute' the intensity, so to speak, with exposure control. Under- and over-exposure can make a great deal of difference to the appearance and the feelings expressed in a picture. Any colour is intensified, or given a stronger colour saturation, by slight under-exposure on slide film, or over-exposure on negative emulsion. On some films, you can vary this by as much as two stops, but you should experiment with your favourite emulsion first to find out. You can de-saturate colours with over-exposure for slides and under-exposure for prints. Paler colours, particularly pastel shades, respond more dramatically to exposure shifts than do stronger colours. Therefore, only a slight exposure manipulation is required to maintain the delicate values whilst altering their visual and emotional intensity.

Light itself is a great means of colour control. Like tones, hues are affected by the distance from the subject and/or the intensity of the illumination. Bring the light close and the hue brightens to become more intense; move it away, or reduce the light's intensity, and you subdue the colour for a more sombre visual statement.

Relating colours

Now, the difficulty is that there are not too many opportunities for separating the colours in a scene and making use of only one or two. Every colour is invariably surrounded by other colours and/or tones. This sets up special relationships which can actually alter as certain colours meet other colours. For instance, the very intensity of some colours – such as reds, oranges, and yellows – makes them stand forward. Wherever they are placed; whatever their surroundings, they command attention by suggesting strength.

However, these brilliant hues can overwhelm the others

easily. If there is too much or too many in a picture, the brain rebels and tells the eye to look somewhere else. They must be used in small doses except for the occasional special effect. Where they really score is when you photograph a scene which is almost monochromatic – such as the greens of a landscape, or the greys of a cityscape. Use a single – even small – strong colour within the scene and you get a very strong visual impact. Red, or orange, for instance, on dark grey or black is stunning. The colours appear to be even more saturated and strong to harmonise well with the dark, melodramatic values.

By and large, bright colours look best on a dark background, and vice versa. However, strange things happen to them both emotionally and visually. As always happens with contrast situations, the proximity of the tones or colours cause both to be intensified. Moreover, they appear to change in size too. It is only a visual illusion, of course, but if you use a single strong colour in front of a white or light ground, it appears to be smaller. Turn it around, and the reverse is true.

Where objects are the same size, those of the stronger hue overshadow the weaker. They seem to be larger. Thus, you must balance colours just as you do tones and shapes. By the selection of a thoughtful viewpoint, you can emphasise or subdue certain parts of the same scene and cause certain hues to be dominant, or include more of them. That is the way to make sure your viewers share in your emotional experience. In addition, you can use focusing and controlled shutter speeds to give you the equivalent of the artist's palette. When colours go out of focus, the edges merge and blend to produce quite different hues. Where they are completely out of focus, or heavily blurred, the change is radical. Reds and blues merge to become purples; yellows and blues become greens, and so on.

Colour control, then, is all about the positive use of the colours you see in the scene. You must be prepared to make the changes necessary to achieve the feelings you experienced, or wish to convey. Look at the scene then, observe the colours, and decide how you are going to photograph them. Pointing and pressing haphazardly is out.

No time for dithering about with settings in a shot like this. You have to know which way the focusing turns to keep the image sharp and you must have the settings fixed in advance.

Chapter Three The Subject

1

Action

In this section you bring all the theories you have learned so far into practice. Action photography is the first stepping stone. The title conjures up impressions of racing cars, sprinters, and the like. Yet it really applies to any movement, not only on the part of the subject but also on your part: the speed with which you can get your camera into action, properly set for the conditions and subject.

Your speed is governed by how well you know the fundamentals of using your camera. If you have to dither about to get the facts right before you can turn your attention to the subject, it will be gone. Action hangs about for no one. You have to be ready. For instance, do you know, without looking, which way your focusing ring turns for infinity? Could you adjust the exposure, without checking your meter, for that open shade, or that deep shadow you can see right now? If you want to excel at action, you should know – then your subconscious can take care of it in the field, and leave you to concentrate on the subject.

Getting good action shots is mostly a matter of anticipation. Anticipate the variety of lighting conditions a moving subject might pass through – or through which you might pass, hunting for it – meter them, and you will know what to do when it happens. You will not have to refer to your meter again for exposure settings.

Keep it sharp

Trying to keep a fast-moving subject in focus is another matter, however. Following it is no good. More often that not you will be focussed somewhere else when the action comes to a crisis. What makes more sense is to get to know something about the activity so that you can judge in advance where the action hot-spots are likely to be. Before it begins, focus on those areas and mark the footages with small pieces of tape. Then when things begin to move in any one of those directions you can turn to the appropriate tape and wait for it to come to you.

If it is you that is moving about, trying to catch some interesting action on the hop, pre-focus on 15ft and set as small an aperture as you can. When you see a subject, walk forward until it is in focus (if it is not already) and let the depth of field take care of the rest.

Speed setting

Striking the right balance between depth of field and shutter speed is difficult. You naturally want a fast shutter but that means a wide aperture and a limited depth of field. Add to this the probability that you are using a telephoto lens to fill the frame and you are not going to have much depth to play with.

The answer then is to choose a shutter which just matches the action. Not everything has to be 'frozen' with 1/1000th sec. If a slower speed will stop movement just as well, use it. The re-adjusted aperture will improve the depth of field as a result.

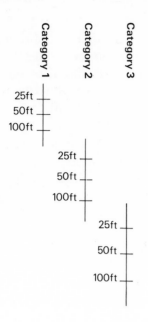

Category 1 · Category 2 · Category 3

25ft
50ft
100ft

25ft
50ft
100ft

25ft
50ft
100ft

Directions:

Place a ruler on the pivot point at the top left corner and lay it across the category line and relevant distance. Then check the shutter speed required in the correct subject direction line.

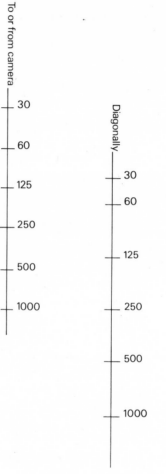

To or from camera

30
60
125
250
500
1000

Diagonally

30
60
125
250
500
1000

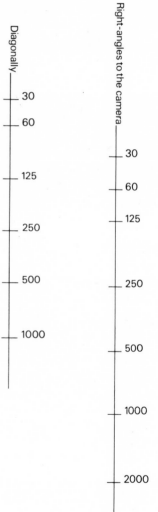

Right-angles to the camera

30
60
125
250
500
1000
2000

Category 1

Walking people and animals

Playing children

Workers

Boats

Category 2

Athletics

Point-to-point and horse races

Fast boats

Skiing

Surfing

Skating

Category 3

Trains

Racing cars and bikes

When subjects are moving directly towards or away from you, they can be 'stopped' with relatively slow shutter speeds. 1/125th sec. was all that was required here.

There are three factors to be taken into account when making decisions about shutter speeds – subject movement, distance, and movement direction. For instance, it seems right that a runner will not require as fast a shutter as the High Speed Train. However, if the runner is passing right in front of the lens, and the train is on the horizon, the reverse is true. It could mean 1/500th sec. for the runner, and 1/125th sec. for the train. Even if they are the same distance away, the required 1/500th sec. for the runner will probably still be too much for the train if it is coming straight at you. Before you jump out of the way the same 1/125th sec. will be enough. If it is moving diagonally, then perhaps 1/250th sec. will be needed. Study the chart opposite which gives subjects, angles of movement and shutter speeds, and commit them to memory for use in the field.

Blurred images

The chart only gives suggested shutter speeds for main body movement. Arms, legs, wheels, and so on, move faster. But, to 'freeze' them with a fast shutter destroys all sense of movement. It is true that the attitude of a running figure, even if completely stopped by the shutter, is enough. But a vehicle will look as though it was standing still if everything is needle sharp. Choose a slow enough speed to permit the wheels to blur and the impression of movement is strong.

Some photographers allow everything to blur. As long as it is vaguely recognisable, it certainly gives the image a sort of frenetic activity. However, the right effect is not easy to achieve and it is best to use limited blur at first.

Panning is one way of producing exciting effects with blur. As the subject comes into view, pick it up in the viewfinder

The panning action causes everything else but the subject to be blurred and creates a marked impression of speed. You can see this also in the picture of the motor cyclist on p.23.

and follow it. As it arrives at the point opposite where you have pre-set the focus, shoot. However, do not stop the camera's movement. Continue to follow the subject in a smoooth action until the shutter has settled down again. If you get it right, the subject itself is sharp but it is surrounded by blurred speed lines because nothing else was moving at the same speed.

You can pan in any direction – horizontally, vertically, or whatever. Try it on pole vaulters, sky divers, and children on the helter-skelter. In low light situations, panning is most useful.

Slow and sharp

Moments occur in every activity where a slow shutter speed will stop everything – and still show action. First, when a person leaps into the air to head a ball, dive from a board, or clear a hurdle, there is a split second when his or her upward movement ceases. Gravity takes over and they start to fall. In that instant, there is no movement and you can 'freeze' everything with 1/30th sec.

Second, at the end of a violent action, there is little or no movement, but all the earmarks of activity are there. Try catching a golfer at the end of a swing, or a discus thrower at the moment it leaves his hand, or any other such activity. You will only need 1/60th sec.

Another means of stopping action with a slower shutter than usual is to take advantage of the law of movement. Choose a viewpoint where most of the action is moving towards or away from you. It makes doubly good sense at such events as basketball, or football, and the like, because most of the excitement takes place around the goals. You will be right there to catch it.

A long jumper moves forward at high speed, but all other bodily movements have more or less ceased and it is possible to 'freeze' it all with a relatively slow shutter speed.

Timing

Catching an action highlight at the right moment is not easy. Some new cameras have auto wind facilities which permit continuous shooting at some 2 or 5 frames per second (fps). They certainly give you a better chance to get the timing right, but even they are no substitute for observation. Learn to see the signs. When you can anticipate an exciting happening far enough in advance, you will be ready to capture it with just one shot.

Action supplement: flash photography

A sure way of stopping action is to use a flash gun. The light is so intense and brief that falling water is 'frozen' and bullets are stopped dead.

In fact, flash has many uses other than stopping action. Its main purpose is to illuminate where not enough light exists. But in order to use it effectively, for whatever purpose, it is necessary to understand something about it.

There are two types – bulb and electronic. Small though they are, flash bulbs emit an extremely bright light. They are filled with fine aluminium wire which is ignited by a charge of electricity. All of its power and light is put into that one short, sharp, intense flash. After that it is dead. Normally they are coated blue to raise the colour temperature of the light to match a daylight colour film.

Long life flash

The electronic gun differs from the bulb in that it has a tube which is filled with Xenon gas. The light tends to be much briefer, although generally not as intense, and the tube can be used again and again. The batteries recharge the power in a few seconds after each flash, and it is ready again for action.

As a flash gun is a point light source, its distance from the subject is very important. The light cannot, of course, be measured with an ordinary meter, so you have to resort to mathematics. Each gun or bulb is given a Guide Number (GN). It is based on the power of the flash bulb plus the sensitivity of the film. Match GN to your film speed and then divide into it the aperture you have chosen. The answer is the distance from the subject you should position your gun.

If distance is important, divide it into the GN and it will give you the aperture you should use.

In the first instance, it might be:

$$\frac{32}{f4} = 8ft$$

In the second, it might be:

$$\frac{20}{8ft} = 2\tfrac{1}{2}, \text{ or } 2.5 - f2.8 \text{ is the nearest}$$

Sometimes, these days, GNs are worked out for use with metres instead of feet. Get that sorted out before you start, or you will get some hopelessly wrong answers.

With a computerised electronic flash gun it is possible to 'freeze' falling water. Hold the gun really close and the sensor will shut off the flash after an exposure of only 1/50,000th sec. or thereabouts.

Automatic flash

Many modern electronic guns have a special auto feature which obviates all this. An electric eye just below the flash tube collects the light reflected from the subject and shuts the gun off when it estimates the subject has had enough. Some even save the unused power and feed it back into the system for shorter re-cycling times and longer battery life. This is called a Thryster Circuit.

Many have several auto settings for a variety of light strengths. All you do is set the film speed on the auto calculator fixed to the gun, and that indicates the aperture you should use and the maximum distance from the subject the gun can be used. Within that maximum you can fire it from any distance you like without having to make any re-calculations.

Synchronisation

The shutter does not really come into flash calculations because, when the flash is the main light source, its brief light acts as a shutter. For instance, if your shutter is 1/60th sec., and your flash is 1/10,000th sec. (quite common with electronic guns), the subject will receive only 1/10,000th sec. of exposable light.

The important thing about the shutter speed is that it should uncover the entire film frame at once. Between the lens shutters do this at every speed. But focal plane types only open fully at the slower speeds – 1/60th sec. and below for horizontally working shutters, and 1/125th sec. on those which work vertically. At faster speeds than those, the frame is exposed by a travelling slit.

However, if your shutter is too slow, a secondary, or ghost image may record. This will be a blur in a fast-moving subject, and another sharp but less distinctive image in a still one. This is because the ambient light level is high enough to permit the shutter to form its own image.

Flash in practice

Avoid using the flash gun fixed to the camera. The lighting is very flat and results in lack of modelling and heavy rim shadows. Moreover, subjects looking directly into the flash at the time of exposure suffer deadness of the eyes with monochrome film, and redness with colour. The problem is solved by moving the flash gun away from the camera.

You will have to get an extension cable. This fits in between the coaxial socket on the camera and the short cable on the gun. Now you can hold the gun out at arm's length, high and to one side, to approximate the ideal 45° lighting. In one move you will eliminate the eye problem and produce good modelling to boot.

Bounce flash

However, flash off-camera will still not get rid of the heavy shadows. To do that you will have to diffuse the light. This can be effected by covering the tube with a thickness of white handkerchief, but the light output is cut down by one stop.

A more flexible method is to bounce the light from a ceiling or wall. Your distance for calculation is now from the flash gun to the bounce surface, and then on to the subject. Add it all up and divide it into the GN. When you have the new aperture, open it up by one more stop to compensate for absorption by the bounce surface (for a dark one, make it two stops). The resultant lighting is softer and more even.

You can only use your computer for bounce lighting if the flash head moves independently of the electric eye. The auto unit has to receive information from the subject and if it is pointed at the ceiling, it cannot.

Balanced flash

When you use a flash gun, you must take into account the natural light already there. By ignoring it you are likely to get a well-exposed subject in total darkness. Indeed, you may want to photograph someone in front of a window – and see the view as well; or watching television – and see what is on. Finding the right balance is a question of marrying the two lights.

Start by taking an exposure reading of the scene. Base that reading on a shutter speed which synchronises with flash. In the case of television, it will have to be 1/30th sec.: the scanning line takes that long to make a complete picture. Now, take the aperture given and divide that into the GN, or use it for setting the right auto mode. The two lights are now matched.

With this basic method under your belt, you can adapt it to give you more light or less when you want to alter the lighting balance for some reason. One or two are explored in later chapters.

Finally, a word of warning about GNs and manufacturer's calculations. They are based on use in the average light room. You will rarely encounter the same conditions and since the subject is illuminated by light spill bouncing from ceiling and

Balanced lighting is important when you want to retain atmosphere. It would have been a shame to destroy the night lighting in this shot, so the exposure setting for the flash was based on the readings taken from the shop window. Even then, a distance was carefully chosen so as not to destroy the existing shadows.

walls, as well as direct flash, the size and colour of the room makes a difference.

You will have to undertake tests in a variety of conditions to make sure you can get the exposure right when it matters. Simply take some test shots in all types of places you are likely to encounter – including out of doors – using the manufacturer's recommendations, and then one or two stops either side (bracketing), without altering the flash/subject distance. Keep notes so that when you see the results, you can identify the correctly exposed negative immediately.

3

Nature

If you are ever stuck for something to photograph, walk into a nearby wood. It could be a local park, or the open country-side; in any event, the subjects are boundless. Those same subjects are continually changing, too; the stark shapes of Winter, sometimes covered in snow, and Spring heralding new life with blossoms, new buds, and emerging wildlife. In Summer you have bright sun with fully open flowers, etc., while Autumn brings frosts and mists. And in every season you will find people there.

Woodland subjects

One of the first things you will notice is that it is necessary to work very close to the subject. You are hemmed in on all sides by undergrowth but a careful examination reveals much of interest.

Look for special lighting on trees and leaves which pick out their textural qualities. Note, too, the translucence of leaves, particularly when they are wet, as the sun backlights them. An exposure reading direct from the leaf – making sure the sun does not find the cell – is all that is necessary. However, bracket the exposure by one or two stops just to make sure.

Leaves, flowers, and ferns all make delightful shapes when photographed in isolation but it is not easy to separate them from the background. If it is in shadow and the subject is brightly lit, you will get sufficient contrast. But, as nature is somewhat disorderly, the odd bits that stick out everywhere pick up light and show up as distracting highlights. If you feel destructive, break away all the offending bits. A better method, however, is to supply your own background – your jacket, or a piece of plain paper.

A neutral colour or tone looks more natural but, on some occasions, a contrasting one creates useful visual shock. A black card behind a white flower delineates the shape clearly and makes it stand out dramatically. With colour, you have quite a wide choice. Green, for instance, is a natural backdrop for any colour; a yellow flower against blue, contrasts; a red one against that same blue harmonises, and so on.

Avoid pictures of vast tracts of multi-coloured flowers. Too many colours in any one picture tend to overwhelm. Pick out instead areas of the same colour, or even single blooms. Remember, simplicity is the key. Often, the full potential of a subject cannot be seen with the naked eye. Use your tele-photo or tele-extender and select likely subjects here and

there for closer examination and you will find a great deal of detail ripe for commitment to film.

In the open spaces of heathland and parks, there is no difficulty with exposure, but step in under the trees of a wood and the light level drops alarmingly. This makes fast film and a tripod standard equipment.

Wild life

A fast film is immensely valuable when you stalk wild life. You can get some great photographs but creatures in the wild are incredibly difficult to capture on film. Waits of several hours are the norm, watching squirrels or rabbits, or birds through a long telephoto, willing them to come into the right position or a better light. Many times the wait is in vain but when they do, their movements are so fast and erratic that only a fast film will give you a suitable shutter speed.

Early morning is the best time. They are out on their foraging expeditions and there are not too many people around. Find the animal runs and gathering places, and lie in wait for them as far away as your lens will allow.

Of course, the best thing is a hide. These are virtually little cabins with a hole for the lens to poke through so you are hidden from the direct view of your subject. It is usually left in position for days before use, so the creatures can investigate and subsequently dismiss it. Then you can get to work. It is not a thing for the casual cameraman but if you are at all serious about photographing wild life, you ought to consider building one.

In the garden

A surprising amount of wild life gathers around houses, particularly birds. A few bits of bread entices them and you can then use your house as a hide and shoot from the comfort of an armchair. However, if you are too close to the subject and the window is open, you need a quiet camera. The SLRs instant return mirror makes so much noise that the birds are in flight before the shutter fires. It will pay you to clean your windows well and shoot through them – even though glass does degrade images.

Your own pets are good to practise on, although they are not generally as timid, to gain experience of what is involved. They, like any other creature, can be enticed with food to where you want them to be. This does not limit you with poses. Watch an animal or bird eat. They are continually bobbing up and down, watching for danger, fighting off interlopers, and a host of other things. There is a feast of pictures to be had.

Wild life is not all that easy to photograph unless you are serious about it and go to great lengths to get all the right equipment. However, if you lie in wait long enough, with a long lens, you can capture some interesting pictures of the less timid creatures.

The effect of atmosphere and UV light is quite clear in this picture. Note how the background is bluish and somewhat indistinct when compared with detail in the foreground. A filter does help – here a Skylight filter was used – but sometimes the effect helps the picture to seem more real.

It is important to make sure you use the film meant for the colour temperature in which you are shooting. However, on many occasions this is not possible. A filter will alter the colour balance to make it more nearly like that of the original, but you might also like to experiment to see if the effect enhances the subject. In this picture a daylight film was used under shop window lighting with no filter.

*Contrast in colour is managed by
putting next to each other primaries
and their complementaries.*

When shooting through wire cages at zoos and wildlife parks, use a wide aperture, press the lens right up to the cage, and let the minimal depth of field make the cage 'disappear'. It will be so far out of focus it will not register.

Captive wild life

A zoo or wild life park will give you opportunities to photograph creatures not readily available in our countryside. Their confinement does not make the job any easier and you still have to have your wits about you.

Feeding time is a good time to catch them. If you ask the keeper nicely he might give or throw the food into a favourable position for your camera.

The bars or wire cages will cause you some problems. Where it is safe, you can shoot between the bars; where it is not you will simply have to feature them as a part of the composition. Wire cages are a different matter. Place the lens, where you can, right on the cage and use a small aperture. This enables you to shoot through the wire squares. Where the light does not permit a small aperture, open it right up so the depth of field is wafer thin. Any wires in front of the lens are then thrown so far out of focus they will not even register.

4
Nature supplement: close-ups

Close-up photography brings you another world of subjects. When you examine quite ordinary objects through a close-up device you will see all kinds of possibilities – like this saw-tooth appearance of a stinging nettle. Note the tiny depth of field when working at such close distances.

There are a number of devices available which enable you to get closer to nature and other subjects than the 18in. minimum focus on your standard lens. They bring them up to life size (called close-ups) and beyond (macrophotography).

Magnifications of the image size are given as a ratio. 1:1 is life size; 2:1 is twice life size; and 1:2 is half life size. Beyond 10:1 the job is simplified with a microscope and you are into microphotography.

The simplest device for getting nearer to the subject is a close-up lens. It screws on the front of a lens like a filter and is measured in dioptres. A No. 1 dioptre more or less halves the closest focusing distance; a No. 2 halves that one; and so on. The maximum you can get is 10 dioptres.

Backward lenses

Beyond this point, something more complex than a simple close-up lens is needed. In fact, you would get better results by mounting another standard lens in reverse on the one on-camera. Indeed, a lens reversed directly on the camera makes a good close-up device. You do need an adaptor but a standard lens will give sharper close-up results this way.

The basic problem is that you lose the auto aperture. An inexpensive pin depressor holds it down so that you can operate the aperture by hand if the lens does not have a

The Polysales Z ring fitted between lens and close-up tubes.

manual switch. However, auto facilities can be retained with a Z ring. This is a device which fits to the rear end of the lens and operates the aperture and shutter with a double cable release.

Of course, if you have a macro lens, most of this can be obviated. A simple switch-over device turns it from a standard fixed focal length lens or zoom into a close-up lens. In fact, the title 'macro' is a little misleading. They very rarely go as far as 1:1.

Extension rings

A popular accessory which fits between the lens and the camera body to extend the distance and permit closer focusing. A set consists of three rings, 12mm, 20mm, and 36mm in depth. They can be used either separately or in any combination, depending on how much magnification you require. All together, they achieve a magnification ratio of 1:1.25 – more than life size. Most permit full auto aperture facilities.

Because you have extended the lens/film distance, the light has further to travel. As a result, it is less bright at the film plane and you must compensate in your exposure calculations. A TTL meter will do that automatically, otherwise you have to resort to mathematics.

The calculation is:

$$\frac{\text{actual aperture x lens/film distance}}{\text{lens focal length}}$$

The answer is the equivalent aperture. For example:

$$\frac{\text{f8 x 36mm}}{52\text{mm}} = 5.5$$

or, the nearest aperture, f5.6, indicates that there is one stop light loss with this tube.

Close-up bellows

A similar situation exists with extension bellows. They too fit behind the lens and require exposure compensation – using the same formula – but they have the advantage of being continuously variable. When you want to alter magnification with the rings, you have to unscrew (or unbayonet) the lens, fit a new extension, then put it all back together again. On the bellows, you simply alter the extension by rotating a wheel. More importantly, bellows extend further than rings and give greater magnifications.

Unfortunately, bellows which permit auto aperture control are expensive. You may have to make do with a non-auto set and operate the aperture manually. Alternatively, you can fit your Z ring between the bellows and lens and operate everything in unision with a double cable release.

Any of these close-up devices can be used in combination with any of the others for greater magnifications. As long as you obey the rules of usage – exposure adjustments, etc. – your results will be perfectly acceptable.

Keeping steady

When you get close to a subject, not only is it magnified, but so is the camera movement. Those devices which require exposure compensation aggravate the situation by often demanding very slow shutter speeds. A tripod and cable release then has to be used.

Fixing the camera on a tripod is useful for another reason. The closer you get to a subject, the smaller the area the lens covers. If you move the camera it is not always that easy to find again. A tripod solves the problem.

Live subjects

An inanimate object is not too difficult to photograph close-up, but a living insect has to be kept still long enough to get a sharp picture.

Food comes to the rescue again. A heavily pollinated flower, or something sweet, like glucose, works well with most. If you can find out your subject's most favourite dish, so much the better. However, even when it is chomping away merrily, an exposure of one second is hardly going to freeze it. Therefore, you need plenty of light.

Good, strong sunlight may be sufficient. As it is coming from one direction, you will need a reflector to fill in heavy shadows. A better alternative, though, are photofloods. Use one as a key light – to provide basic illumination and modelling – and another at a greater distance to brighten shadows.

Even living subjects stand up well to the close-up treatment. Here a flash was used to give enough light to permit the use of three extension tubes behind a 250mm telephoto lens.

Close-up flash

The strongest light of all is thrown by flash and, being fast, freezes an insect's most frantic movements. The problem is that you cannot see what it is going to do. Therefore, you must experiment, taking plenty of pictures with flash guns at different distances and positions. Again, you will need a reflector to fill in, or another flash gun.

You can use flash to capture close-up and macro subjects out of doors too. Fix your main gun on a flash bracket adapted to point at nearby subjects. Put the second, less powerful gun in the accessory shoe for fill-in.

If both guns are of equal strength, cover one with a white handkerchief to reduce its power by one stop (or two thicknesses for two stops). Both guns can be fired simultaneously with a multiple flash socket.

5
People

The most challenging photographic subjects are people. They get up to all sorts of interesting antics as they go about their daily lives – at play, work, rest, or just plain going.

Some of your most rewarding results will come from pictures taken when the subject is unaware. 'Candids' catch them when they are unguarded and most natural. When your subject is absorbed in doing something interesting, such as concentrating on choosing something to buy, or giving directions, or arguing, then is the time to put him on film. Moments of stress are particularly fruitful. You do not have to chase ambulances to find it. Stress occurs when your subject is trying to lift a heavy box, or riding on a Ferris Wheel at the fair.

Candid work is closely akin to action photography. All the same rules apply. Keep your camera at the ready at all times – focused on 15ft, and shutter and aperture set for the prevailing light. Make sure you know, too, what adjustments to make if you find your subject in shade, back or side lighting, then you can shoot 'from the hip' so to speak.

Candid pictures can be secured anywhere. The best people-pictures are possible when the subject is occupied or under stress – as here on the fair 'twister'. The facial expressions tell the story. A pity more of the 'twister' was not included to make clearer what is going on.

Out of sight

A telephoto is a candid photographer's best friend. You can stay well back and remain unnoticed, yet still fill the frame. Do not choose one which is too long though, or your depth of field will be too short and you may end up with a string of 'face' pictures. It is important to see what they were doing. Moreover, a long lens puts too much distance between you and the subject and passers-by will continually obscure your view.

Natural obstacles like doorways, windows, parked cars, etc., provide good cover. If you want to get closer, then move towards the subject behind other pedestrians. But all that might be unnecessary. If your prey is totally absorbed in what he is doing, he will not even notice you.

Portraits

When you take pictures of people who are aware of you, there are a whole set of other problems to deal with.

Posing is the first one. Avoid the standing-to-attention formal poses and try to make things look more natural. Plenty of chat with lots of questions go a long way towards relaxing your subject and make him or her feel at ease. Study pictures taken by professionals for ideas. Copy them. Soon, lots of adaptations and new ideas will occur to you and your pictures will take on a more original slant.

By and large, have the subject look directly into the lens. This provides eye-contact in the print and makes it more memorable to the viewer. However, do not pose the subject square-on to the camera. This pose thickens the face and body to rugby player proportions. Use three-quarter and side views instead, with the head turned towards the camera. Three-quarter face views are most suitable for head and shoulder shots. It slims down round faces too. Profiles offer a chance of doing something different but if your sitter has a long nose, make it full face instead.

For this kind of portrait, your camera has to be close. Four feet is the minimum, and the camera should be level with the sitter's eyes. If you approach any closer the face appears to be distorted – this is called foreshortening. Nose, forehead and jaw become bulbous and ears disappear around the side of the head. A safer way is to move further back and fit a short telephoto lens.

Natural lighting

Direct sunlight – even when it is at 45° – is not conducive to good outdoor portraiture. Shadows are heavy and awkward and require considerable fill-in from a reflector or flash.

Flash is particularly useful for relieving shadows but if you balance the lighting exactly – as described earlier – they will disappear altogether. The ideal ratio, you will remember, is 2:1 for colour, and 4:1 for monochrome and that is as deep as the shadows ought to go.

One or two thicknesses respectively over the flash tube will cut the intensity to the correct level or, alternatively, you can adjust your calculations. Simply choose a GN which represents a stop or two faster film – e.g. 800, or 1600 ASA instead of 400 ASA.

If you have a computer gun with several auto settings for different light intensities, use the distance for the strongest power with an actual light intensity of one or two stops weaker. Make sure, however, that the electric eye is not pointed straight into the sun. It could mistake the sun for the light it is waiting for and cut the flash off too early.

Open shade is a much more practical portraiture proposition. In the shade of a wall, for instance, the subject still receives illumination from the open sky. But it is much softer and more flattering. Where there is no suitable open shade, have your subject turn her back to the sun and photograph the shadow side.

In either case, make sure you read the shadows only. For extra detail and a light summery appearance, open the aperture by an extra stop, or even two. Should the shadows be too heavy and demand a very slow shutter speed, fill them in with a reflector or flash.

Move the subject into full shade and you will not only get the same soft, flattering lighting but also the opportunity of being creative with backgrounds. You will have to use a wide aperture because of the low light. The resultant narrow depth of field then throws everything immediately behind the subject totally out of focus. Where the landscape outside of the shade is brightly lit, it will contrast dramatically with the subject, and the woolliness from being unsharp will invoke a strong impression of a summery day.

Backgrounds in general are important in portraiture. Out of doors there can be so many distractions and, if they cannot be thrown out of focus, it is often necessary to cut them out altogether. Shoot from a low angle and you get the plain sky as a backdrop; get up high, and the ground seems to surround the subject.

Windowlight

This is an excellent form of portrait illumination. Moreover, since the best lighting comes from overcast or rainy days, it allows you to take pictures when it might otherwise not be possible. Indeed, bright sunlight is not at all the best for windowlight pictures. The contrast is much too great.

Do not pose the subject, in any light, too close to the window. Rather, sit him well into the room and beyond the window. Then the subject will be illuminated from the front and side and the contrast is reduced to manageable proportions.

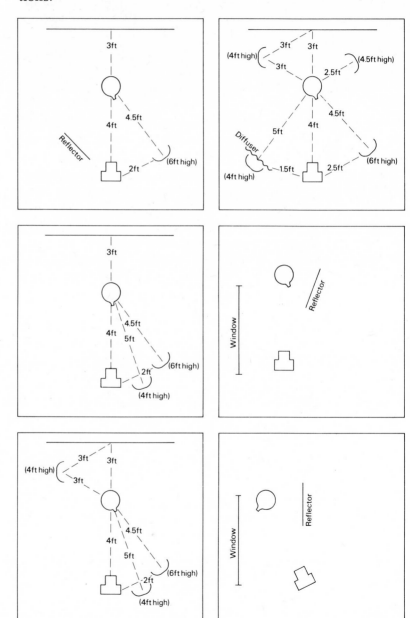

Photoflood and window lighting chart

Window light is kind when used carefully. However, close to the window the contrast is great and you may need to fill in the shadows with a reflector. Here it was not necessary as the face was pointing at the light source.

In the studio

Much more precise control is possible with photofloods. You can start with one 500 watt flood and a reflector. Two is better, and three, plus a 250 watt hair light, is ideal.

Clear a space of about 8ft by 6ft in your living room and set up a plain, uncreased background – a sheet is fine – at one end. Position a backless stool 3ft in front of that and your camera on a tripod (at eye height) some 4ft in front of that.

Set up your main light 4½ft from the subject and 2ft wide of the camera, at a height of 6ft. If it is your only lamp, get a friend to hold a big reflector facing the subject's shadow side. If you have a second lamp, place it between the main light and the camera at about 4ft high and 5ft from the subject. That provides sufficient fill-in.

The great thing about studio lighting is that it is infinitely controllable. You are in command and with a studied approach you can achieve a variety of effects.

The important thing about studio lighting is that, no matter how many lamps you use, there must be only one set of shadows. They are made by your main light. All the other lamps do is lighten existing shadows to the correct ratio, or add highlights to the hair and background.

Use the lighting chart opposite as a guide for further approaches to portraiture. If you do exactly what they say you will get well-lit portraits every time.

Finally, it is important to note that photoflood lamps do not last very long. So, switch them off when you are not actually shooting or checking lighting and exposure. Then, when the session is over, do not move them before they cool down. Sudden jerks could break the filament.

Other than that, portraiture is fun.

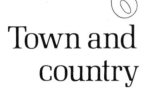

Town and country

After people, the second most photographed subject is scenery. The beauty and ugliness of the world around us has always captured man's imagination and he has spent much time recording it on canvas and film.

Photographing land, sea, and cityscapes is deceptive. It seems as though it ought to be simple enough to point a camera and capture all that breathtaking beauty. But for reasons already explained – picture borders, two-dimensional image, and haze-reduced tonal and colour saturation – much care is required.

Scenery pictures score when they have a centre of interest. There should be some point to the shot beyond a mere record. A centre of interest draws everything else to it and might be a gigantic oak, a farm house, or a flock of sheep. And even when you have discovered the centre of interest, use your viewfinder to find the right angle from which to shoot.

Always begin by assuming you are in the wrong place. That will keep your mind open and prompt you into looking for other other possibilities. Survey the subject from several points of view, watching the changing arrangement of shapes and lines, and what happens to the light and shadows. When you find what you are looking for, walk back and forth along this new line of sight to start the selection process. As things begin to come together, raise and lower the camera height. Eventually, just the right collection of lines, masses, light and shade, will appear in the viewfinder.

Landscapes require careful handling to retain something of their original splendour. The upper third strong line was reserved for the skyline and the quay side and bollard were used as a foreground object. These also serve as an opposing diagonal to the lines of boats, which take the eye through the picture in either direction.

Formal composition

So far, you have been riding on instinct. But do not forget, that has been boosted by the things you learned in Chapter Two, all of which should now be a natural part of your photographic vocabulary. However, it is most important that you employ the strong areas one-third of the way in, vertically and horizontally, for foreground objects and frames, and horizons. Another equally valid system is to divide the picture area into fifths and use those lines for composing sections of the landscape.

Timing plays an important part too. Apart from waiting for moving elements such as people, boats, vehicles, and clouds to get to the right place, you have lighting to consider. Scenery looks better when the shadows are fairly long to break up wide expanses and add modelling. So, if it is not quite right when you are there, wait – or come back later.

A green filter is most useful for the black and white landscape. It separates the various shades of green and 'brings out' the clouds. Stronger results are possible with an orange filter. But if the sea figures largely in your view, as its colour is a reflection of the sky, it will be darkened too, and look unnatural. Orange filters are best saved for townscapes where the darkened sky contrasts markedly with the lightened concrete. A polariser also darkens the sky, for colour as well as monochrome. However, if it is used insensitively, you could take out all the sparkle and life from glass and water in the scene.

Occasionally, use your telephoto for scenery. Because it tends to 'push' the planes together, it turns rolling hills, angular buildings, and the like, into fascinating patterns.

Architecture

Sometimes, parts of the total scene are so interesting that they warrant exploration. It pays to move in close on these occasions and pick out the detail of a photogenic tree, cliff, or building.

When faced with such a tall subject, the natural thing is to point the camera upwards to get the top in. But, in doing so, you have shifted the film plane from the vertical, and the resultant image appears to lean over backwards. To keep it straight, the camera must be upright.

Of course, the ready answer is to move further back. However, this means you will have more foreground to contend with. It can be cut out in the final picture but a more sensible course is to make the foreground count. Use the compositional elements contained within it to lead the eye to the subject. Alternatively, you can raise the level of the camera. Climb a building, or tree, opposite and you will eventually reach a point where you can photograph the entire structure without having to lean the camera over and include so much foreground. Where none of this is possible, give up and move in close to the base of the subject. The extreme shooting angle will converge the verticals dramatically – and make the whole thing look deliberate.

Playing about with perspective in this way can lead to some fascinating results. However, in general shots of buildings, it must be more acceptable. Make sure you can see two sides of the building. They should not be equal. The vanishing points made by the perspective lines of the two walls should form at different points – one within the picture frame, and the other well outside. Head-on views are fine only for rows of arches or doors and the like, where their repetitious, rhythmic shapes form a single point perspective. The arches or doors appear to get progressively smaller right down through the centre of the picture. The effect of dramatic depth is accentuated if the shapes alternate in light and shade.

Buildings have character and it pays to seek it out and try to show it in your pictures. Often, it will best be expressed by isolating a tiny portion of the structure – such as intricate carvings, the lines of bridge supports, and even reflections in

Single point perspectives give a marked impression of depth, especially if, as in this case, the arches alternate dark and light. Then the tonal separation helps to increase the three-dimensionality.

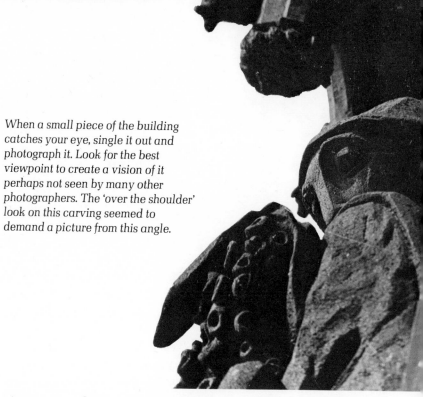

picture windows. Use your telephoto lens, or a zoom, to single out these items. It will help you to explore areas of the structure which are otherwise inaccessible, and build up images of all that is interesting about it, piece by piece.

In the dark

When you have finished your daylight photography, come back at sunset. The spectacular colours add excitement to the most mundane scenes. To get good colour saturation, expose for the sunset and allow everything else to go into silhouette. Whatever the direct reading, bracket your exposures well each side.

Sunsets work best when there is some water in the scene to reflect the colours, or with an interesting shape silhouetted against it. If that interesting shape is important and you want to show detail, use flash. The standard light balancing technique works fine.

As darkness beings to fall, everything takes on a new look – and it is photographable. Perhaps the most exciting places to be at night with a camera are in cities and towns. The twinkling lights and dark shapes of buildings even make a slum look fascinating.

Dusk is the best time. Then the room lights turn buildings into Christmas trees and yet there is still sufficient skylight to delineate the buildings; they do not disappear into a general mass of black.

Long exposures of several seconds are the norm for night photography. Moving lights on cars, Ferris Wheels, fireworks, etc., carve fascinating trails across the emulsion.

It is no good, though, simply pointing the meter at the scene and hoping for the best. It will read only the lights and push everything else down the scale to sink into inky blackness. A good starting point would be to try to read some of the darker areas. At least then, you will get some detail in there.

If your meter is not sensitive enough to handle it, read instead a white card – or the lights themselves. Then, recognising that the shadows need 'pulling up', open the aperture by a further four (or five) stops. The highlights are then pushed up the scale, and the darker areas brought within reach of the latitude of your film.

The chart below will serve as a guide to night exposure, but it should not be taken as gospel. Use it as a guide only and bracket your exposure to make sure you get the results you are after.

Night exposure guide
(all exposures have been based on the use of a 400 ASA film)

Subject	*Estimated shutter speed and aperture* (bracket liberally and make your own tests)
Room light	1/30th sec. at f2.8
Indoor arena	1/125th sec. at f2.8 (directly under lights)
Street/neon lighting	1/30th sec. at f5.6 (for the lights)
	5 secs. at f2 (for shadow detail)
Illuminated buildings	1/30th sec. at f5.6
Illuminated shop windows	1/60th sec. at f4
Fireworks	1 sec. at f8
Fairs	1/30th sec. at f8 (for the lights)
	5 secs. at f2 (for shadow detail and light trails)

As before, do not shoot every night picture from the distance. Get in amongst the activity and shoot illuminated shop windows, the Mods' coffee shop, punk discos, and young lovers under street lamps. Wet streets will make the job easier. They add more sparkle with reflections from the lights, and boost the overall level of illumination for faster shutter speeds. Mist and fog add mystery as streets disappear, people emerge, and the lighting itself can be seen as visible rays.

Film at night

Night photography demands the use of a fast film. But where higher shutter speeds are needed you can increase the basic sensitivity of the film by special exposure and development procedures. It does mean increased grain, but that only adds to the atmosphere of the night.

Night photography in cities and towns can be exciting. The street fair here makes excellent material, providing spectacular lights, while the remaining light in the sky made sure that background buildings stood out clearly. Note how the long exposures have turned individual lights into 'trails', and how the speed pushing has increased grain for a special 'gritty' appearance.

All you are really doing is under-exposing by a known amount and over-developing – or using a vigorous developer – to compensate. Speed increases of 2 and 3 stops are possible in this way. Naturally, you cannot expect optimum results. A film is always at its best when used at the proper speed. However, when the light is so low you cannot get a picture in any other way, film speed pushing comes in very handy. Full details of speed pushing developing procedures are outlined on pp. 118-9.

An interesting situation occurs when you have to use long exposures. When an image is put on film at any speed, it starts to deteriorate immediately. If the exposure takes a long time – say several seconds – the image build-up is so slow that it is actually held back by the natural deterioration. As a result, you need a longer exposure than that indicated to get the right negative density.

The problem has a name. It is called 'reciprocity failure'. On black and white film it can be countered simply by adding to the exposure. On colour, however, you have an additional problem. Not only is there a time lag, but the separate emulsions respond differently and shift the colour balance.

In practice, the shift is difficult to determine as the lighting colour temperature rarely matches that of the film anyway. The safest bet with monochrome and colour is to take plenty of pictures at a variety of exposures and then you can be sure of getting results close to the image you have in your mind.

Chapter Four

The Print

1

The negative

A good monochrome or colour negative is the only means of achieving a technically successful picture. It depends on two things – exposure (which controls density) and development (which controls contrast and colour balance).

To recap, the aim of exposure is to allow sufficient light to reach the film to record detail in the shadows without burning out the highlights. The aim of development is to use the right combination of chemicals for the correct time at the proper temperature to produce good highlight density whilst bringing up that shadow detail. Thus it is by exposing for the shadows and developing for the highlights that good contrast and full gradation is achieved.

Negative contrast

During development, the silver halides which have received the greatest exposure (the highlights) begin to change to pure (black) silver right away. Then the middle tones follow, and after that, the lighter shadow areas (remember, the negative tones are reversed). After a while, the silver grains in the shadow areas stop changing because only a few have been exposed. In the highlights, however, a great many have been affected, and they continue to change.

If developed for too long, they would go on changing and make those areas progressively denser. Detail would be swallowed up. The end product would be a negative with shadows as detailed as they would ever be (you cannot develop more detail where none has been recorded) but with highlights so dense that they have blocked out all the detail.

Developer anatomy

Generally speaking, a basic developing solution consists of:

1. A developing agent – e.g. metol – which reduces the silver halides.
2. A preservative – e.g. sodium sulphite – which stops the developing agent from deteriorating too rapidly in oxygen.
3. An accelerator – e.g. borax – which softens the emulsion and speeds up development.
4. A restrainer – e.g. potassium bromide – which prevents the accelerator from causing the reduction of all the negative's halides.

Developers are in powder or liquid form. Examples of powder developers are Kodak D76 and Ilford ID11; typical liquid developers are Kodak HC110 and Paterson Aculux. The former are made up to working solutions with water and either used as is, or in greater dilutions. The latter are concentrates and have to be diluted to a strength suitable for the type of film being processed.

Colour chemicals also come in powder or liquid form. However, they are generally sold as kits containing everything you require for each processing stage. These cannot be used universally, though. A kit usually matches a particular colour film, or type of film. For example, perhaps the most used is the C22 process from Kodak. This kit is only suitable for colour films which specify that they are compatible with this process. Kodak negative films are suitable, of course, but so are many others. Check the literature before you buy a processing kit.

Since developers are diluted to match in-built film contrasts, it follows that they can be made to vary the contrast of a single film. A strong solution increases contrast for pictures taken on a dull day and a weaker one reduces it when you have been shooting in high contrast situations.

Of the two, the latter is more likely and many developers have instructions on higher dilutions. What happens is that the weaker developer soon exhausts itself on the highlights and slows down the reduction process. In the shadows, on the other hand, the developer has less work to do and keeps right on. As a result the shadows and highlights are brought closer together and there is less contrast.

Practical processing

You need:

A daylight film developing tank suitable for the size film you normally shoot.

A good thermometer in Farenheit or Centigrade.

Chemicals For black and white, you need a developer (try D76 for Kodak films; 1D11 for Ilford films; or Paterson Aculux for either as a starter), stop bath, fixer, and wetting agent. For colour (C22) the kit contains developer, bleach, fixer and stabiliser.

Load the film in the developing tank spiral in total darkness. Any backing paper on the film must be removed first. Follow the tank's instructions carefully and you cannot go far wrong. There are two types – those which load from the outer edge of the spiral, and those which load from the centre. There is nothing to choose in performance, although many cameramen feel that the latter is the easier to handle. It is a matter of opinion.

The loaded spiral is then placed in the tank and the lid clipped or screwed on. You can now switch on the room lights.

The next step is to bring all your chemicals and water to the correct temperature – usually 68°F or 20°C, and 100°F or 38°C for colour. As you cannot see how the film is coming along, you have to control things by keeping it immersed for a specific time at a specific temperature.

We have already seen how time and dilution affects development action. Temperature, when it is too high, causes the developer to act more vigorously and rapidly. A low temperature, naturally enough, slows things down. Therefore all three development controls are closely linked and must be known.

The simplest way of bringing a chemical to the right temperature is to immerse the bottle in which it is contained in water. If the water is at the pre-determined temperature, it will soon adjust the chemicals in the bottles. On the other hand, if you are using liquid chemicals which have to be diluted before use, simply use water at the proper temperature.

The first step in development is to pour water into the tank through the hole in the lid. Rap the tank on the table to dislodge air bells from the film and then, with the filler cap in place, up-end the tank and right it again for five seconds each way. This is called agitation and it should be continued for about thirty seconds.

The water pre-soak brings the film and tank to the correct temperature and swells the emulsion so that the subsequent developing bath spreads evenly and quickly.

Pour out the water, drain the tank, and tip in the developer.

Throughout the development time, agitation must be regular. It too affects development. If it is uneven, it shows on the film as streaks. Too much agitation over-develops; too little under-develops; because what you are doing is replacing exhausted developer with fresh. A good general-purpose scheme is to agitate continuously for the first thirty seconds. Give it another five seconds, thirty seconds later, and then five seconds every minute until development time is up.

Some processing kits, particularly colour, have instructions included which suggest different methods. Follow them to the letter. It is vital to get this stage of the process absolutely right to achieve a good negative.

At the end of the time, pour out and drain the developer from the tank.

Pour in the stop bath. If you do not have any, ordinary water does nearly as well. It will not stop development immediately as does a stop bath, but it will slow it down considerably. It must be the same temperature as all the other baths. If you allow the temperature to fluctuate too wildly, the emulsion will stretch and shrink and it will end up covered with unsightly stress marks.

Make sure every bath during processing – even the wash water – is the correct and uniform temperature throughout.

Exposure and development should be so interlinked that sufficient detail is shown throughout and, as near as possible, a full range of tones.

A minute of continuous agitation is sufficient. Pour out and drain.

Next comes fixation. This chemical turns all the unaffected silver salts water-soluble so they can be rinsed away in the final water bath. Thus, there will be no more to turn the image black when it is brought into the light. Agitation is the same as that used for development.

At the end of this stage, the film can be exposed to room light. However, the residue fixer must be washed completely from the film or it will cause stains. If you can run water at 20°C, let it flow into the centre of the spiral – *not directly over the film* – for at least half an hour. Otherwise make several water changes over that half an hour. Change every thirty seconds for the first three minutes; then every minute for the next five minutes, and then every five minutes thereafter.

The final water bath should contain two or three drops of wetting agent in a full tank of water. Hang the film up and dampen a small piece of chamois with water containing the wetting agent to wipe down both side of the film. This will aid even drying and prevent water marks from forming.

The film should be dried in a little-used room which is fairly free from dust – perhaps overnight in the bathroom. Then cut the film up and store it in properly designed negative envelopes.

Colour specifics

The development of colour negative film varies from this only in the number of baths. For instance, the steps in a typical process are:

1. Development
2. Bleach
3. Wash
4. Fixation
5. Wash
6. Stabilisation

Nevertheless, the time/temperature/agitation control must be just as meticulous – perhaps even more so – in order to get contrast and colour balance absolutely correct.

Push processing

Film which has been deliberately under-exposed requires compensatory development to put back local density in the higher tones. For this purpose, there are some specially mixed developers for black and white work, such as Paterson Acuspeed, Ilford Microphen, and Baumann Diafine and Acufine. The alternative – and this is about all you can do with colour – is to increase immersion time in your standard developer.

All that happens, in fact, with speed pushing is that you sacrifice the lower end of the film's latitude in favour of plenty of detail in the upper end of the tonal scale. Where there is little contrast in the scene, the latitude shift does not matter. You can place the lower end on a thin shadow and still have plenty to play with at the top . If there is much contrast, however, you must lose a great deal of shadow detail.

Recognising those limitations, it is possible to push the film speed from – say – 400 ASA to 800 ASA, 1600, or even 3200 by increasing the standard developing time by about 30 per cent

Speed pushing can be used in a variety of circumstances. Here, the film was uprated by a stop – from 400 ASA to 800 ASA – and over-developed by 30 per cent to ensure a fast enough shutter speed to be able to hand-hold a 500mm lens. Grain is very evident, but contrast was cut by printing the picture on a soft paper.

per extra stop. Colour kits usually give specific details about such exposure/development adjustments.

You must appreciate though, that this type of over-development increases negative contrast. In the first instance mentioned above, that is just what you need. A low-contrast scene needs a little extra boost to give it some life. In the second, however, you must avoid it if you can.

Extra dilution helps. Put the two together and the high dilution compensatory action described earlier contains, or even reduces the contrast, despite over-development. Take Kodak D76 as an example. If normal development takes nine minutes, a dilution of five times the working solution demands a multiplication of the time by five. That makes it forty-five minutes. Agitate for the first two minutes continuously and then let it stand for the remainder of the time. The result is a negative of a finely graded range of tones with virtually no grain.

This is not as easy to control in colour, however, since the developer also processes the colours. Any extra dilution over and above that recommended is likely to turn out some highly peculiar colour balances. Unless you are a compulsive experimenter, it is much safer to put up with the extra contrast and try to control it in printing.

2 The transparency

When a negative is reversed to become a positive, you have a slide, or transparency. They are most common in colour, but can also be found in black and white.

All that happens is that the unfixed but stabilised negative is re-exposed to light, or put through a special chemical, at some stage during the processing, which turns all the negative tones and colours into positive ones.

While professionals prefer colour transparencies to prints because of the brilliant and subtle range of colours they are capable of, it has not caught on in such a big way among the 'masses'. Perhaps the idea of having to set up projector and screen puts them off, or maybe it is because transparencies have to be exposed precisely. With a negative, you can right a few minor wrongs during printing. When you expose a slide film, that is it. You have no room for manoeuvre at all.

Nevertheless, the colour transparency has much to commend it over the colour negative. To begin with, you see the

Colourful events such as mock Civil War battles put on by the Sealed Knot Society make ideal material for colour transparencies. When projected onto a screen the results can be spectacular.

When you are faced with large expanses of a single colour, find an object of a contrasting colour to offset it and give the eye something to rest on. This object must then become the main subject, however, since it will attract strong attention.

Neutral colours are very strong in colour pictures. Take black: it not only provides an eye-catching mood, but also strengthens the other colours present. Saturation is deeper and the picture comes up with greater impact. To achieve this effect in this shot, the film was slightly under-exposed.

*You do not have to go for a multitude
of colours in a subject just because
you have a colour film in your camera.
Sometimes, the simplest subjects
are most effective.*

results right away without having to spend out extra cash for prints, or spending hours in the darkroom making your own. Secondly, it is virtually the only form of colour editors will take. Many will not even look at a print.

Thirdly, it is the closest thing available to a universal film. You can print colour from it direct with processes like Ciba-chrome and you can copy transparencies to make mono-chrome or colour negatives. Prints made from these can be almost as good as pictures taken in the normal way.

Processing

Many colour reversal films have a processing charge built in to the purchase price. Some of them, like Kodachrome, have to be returned for processing. However, there are those available for home processing. Among them are Kodak Ekta-chrome, Barfen Colour, and 3M, and processing kits are readily available.

It is vital that you match the kit to the film. They cannot be interchanged at will and even if an independent kit is pur-chased, it cannot be used other than for those films stated in the instructions. if you try to be clever and develop some-thing else, you will be in for a colour shock.

The main disadvantage with home processing is that the chemicals, when made up, last only for a week or two. You have to save up a half a dozen films and process them one after another. Other than that, the processing methods follow closely those described for monochrome above. Again, there are more baths which, with some variations according to the process used, are likely to be:

1. First developer
2. Stop bath
3. Wash
4. Colour developer
5. Stop bath
6. Wash
7. Bleach
8. Fixation
9. Wash
10. Stabiliser

The first development is really a monochrome process. It produces a black and white negative. The colour couplers get to work during the colour development, when it is also reversed. Bleaching converts the silver to a compound which can be dissolved or dyed.

After the film is dry, you cut it into frames and fit each one into a slide mount. These are available in boxes of 36 from

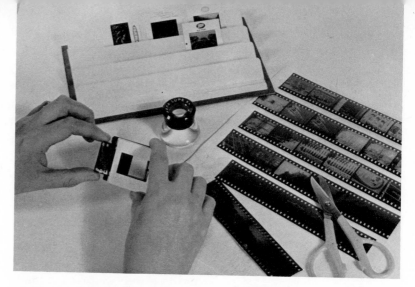

Mount slides in a dust-free situation to make sure they stay clean and unscratched.

photographic dealers. Then store them in boxes or specially designed albums.

When you get a chance, project them onto a good screen and, after everyone has cooed over how lovely they are, study them carefully. Some will obviously be no good, while at the other end of the 'spectrum', one or two may be first class. Put them in a special file for competitions or possible future sales.

Making the black and white print

The final stage is the negative/positive process. If you have done everything you can to produce a good negative, this step will not be too difficult.

All you need for a darkroom is a place which is relatively quiet, and with plenty of running water. The bathroom is ideal. Rudimentary and quite effective blackout can be achieved with a piece of hardboard cut to size and fitted on the inside of the window. Then cover the whole thing with a cut-up dustbin liner.

A heavy curtain outside the door will stop chinks of light creeping in around the edges, and permit exit and entry without admitting too much light. It will also serve as a warning 'flag' to let people know you are in there.

In your darkroom, you need:

An enlarger – sturdy and suitable for monochrome and colour printing
Masking frame – to hold and compose your printing papers
Safelight – one for black and white and one for colour
Three processing dishes and a colour print drum

Print tongs
Printing papers
Thermometer
Chemicals

Getting organised

Start setting things up by placing a large square of wood over the bath as your wet bench. Leave some space at either end to allow access to the water in the bath, used for washing prints. You use the wet bench for developer, wash, and fixer dishes, or to roll your colour print drum about on. Hang your safelight above it.

As a dry bench, use a small table or cupboard. If it is not

It is only by effecting careful processing and accurate printing that you can produce prints with a subtle range of tones matching the original scene.

permanent in the bathroom, it must be sturdy enough not to wobble about when touched. It has to support your enlarger and any table vibration will be transmitted to the enlarger head. The result will be unsharp prints.

Your dry bench needs to be large enough to carry the enlarger, printing papers, negatives, and any other item which must not be mixed with water.

The final requirement is a stool to sit on.

Start making your print by cleaning the negative. A good strong blower will remove most of the dust and if any still persists, use a very clean lens brush. You then place it in the enlarger's negative carrier with the emulsion (dull side) downwards.

Switch the enlarger on.

Enlarger anatomy

Enlarger illumination can take one of two forms. There is the diffuser type where the light from the bulb is scattered by a screen and spread evenly and softly over the lens area, and thus to the paper beneath. The second type uses condensers – like large magnifying glasses – to collect and focus the rays evenly, but somewhat harshly, over the lens area, and on downwards. Some enlargers permit the use of both systems. The condenser enlarger is the most common but the extremely sharp images it produces also emphasise grain and negative blemishes.

The next step is to raise or lower the enlarger head and adjust the masking frame to get the best composition – and then focus. Focusing can be achieved by eye, but a more sure way is to use a magnifier. This is a device which blows up the grain and it is on that which you focus. Your picture could not be any sharper. In either case, to finalise the sharpness, focus on an old piece of enlarging paper. This brings the optically sharp point to the correct level. If it is underneath the magnifier it will produce the same effect.

Next, close the lens aperture down two or three stops to the optimum aperture. The edge of any lens is never optically as good as the centre, and sharper images are possible if you can exclude it. After the optimum aperture, as you close down the aperture still further, it begins to deteriorate again. The second or third stop down from maximum will give you the best image quality.

There are various enlarging meters around which simplify the job of exposure. However, you can do as good a job by making a test strip.

Cut off a strip of printing paper about 8 cm. wide and place it in the masking frame with the enlarger switched off. Make

A typical condenser enlarger.

sure the paper covers an area of the projected image with a full range of tones, particularly black.

With a large card, cover all but one-sixth of the paper in a direction which reveals as many tones as possible over the exposed area. Switch on the enlarger for two seconds, and switch it off. Uncover another sixth and expose that (and the first sixth) for a further two seconds. Continue in this way until the entire paper has been exposed in two-second bands, ranging from 2 seconds to 12.

The paper must now be developed and fixed just like film.

Enlarging paper

This has an emulsion more or less like a film but it is coated on paper. The standard type is divided into contrast grades with Grade 2 being suitable for a negative of a normal contrast. Grades 3, 4 and 5 build up increasing degrees of contrast in images which result from flat, soft negatives. Grades 0 and 1 soften harsh, contrasty images.

Ilford Multigrade does all this on one paper. Grades are changed with the aid of filters positioned above or below the enlarger lens. For normal negatives, no filter is required.

Both types of paper are available as resin coated (RC). This plastic coating keeps them waterproof throughout processing which means that they only need minimal washing at the end and dry very quickly. If you prefer, standard bromide papers are available also. These do get wet, but they are available in a wide variety of surfaces. The RC type is restricted to two or three. Thus, you can print on glossy, silk, matt, pearl, and so on. However, bromide papers are only available in single grades.

You use the time and temperature method for developing all prints. It is usually about 1½ - 2 minutes at 20°C. Rock the dish to make a wave and slip the print into the developer as the wave rushes towards it. That ensures rapid and even coverage. Keep rocking (agitating) the dish for the entire developing time.

Lift the print out of the developer with your print tongs just before the time is up. Handle it only by a corner and allow it to drain. Finally, immerse it in the intermediate wash – or stop bath.

After one minute's continuous agitation, lift out and drain the print again and then immerse it in the fixer. Again, agitate continuously for 3-10 minutes for ordinary fixer (depending on dilution), or for 30 seconds for rapid fix. After the print has drained, rinse it in the bath and take it into ordinary room light.

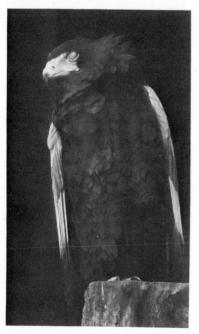

Assessing the test strip

You will see a reproduction of part of the picture divided into six progressively darkened bands. To find the one which shows the brilliance of the correct exposure, look for a black. The first where something which is supposed to be black is black indicates the correct exposure. Before that point, it is grey; after, although it will still be black (for it can get no blacker), the higher values will have been over-exposed and will register lower on the tonal scale than they should be.

Next, look at one of the lighter tones in the correctly exposed strip. Is it too grey? Then you need a harder grade of paper. Where this tone is too light, you must use a softer one.

If you have Multigrade, you can go ahead and make a final print, using the appropriate filter and the adjusted exposure given by the calculator packed with the filters. With ordinary graded stock, you have to make another test strip first, on the new paper.

Develop the print as normal.

Make sure a black is included in the area to be 'test-stripped': at the first point it becomes black on the print, you have the correct exposure time.

Local adjustments

It is possible that some areas of the print will record too dark or too light. It is then necessary to hold back or increase the exposure at those local points.

The first is achieved by cutting a small card to the shape of the offending area. Fix it on a piece of wire and, during the exposure, hold it above the too-dark area. Move it about to prevent a hard edge forming and whisk it away when you think the area has been held back enough. Do not keep it there the entire time or you will get a white space. For an accurate estimate, make a test strip of the area.

To darken a local area, use a large piece of card with a hole cut in it. As it is held in the projected beam from the enlarger, it stops all but the light to the important area. Again, keep it moving. The two techniques are called 'dodging' and 'burning in'.

Prints must be washed for the full time in order to prevent the fixer making stains on them. Ordinary bromide papers require an hour of constantly changed, or running, water. RC papers require only about four minutes.

You can dry your prints laid out on newspapers, picture face up. However, bromide papers curl dramatically and are best dried on a heated dryer. RC papers, being waterproof, dry quicker if they are hung, or stood vertical in a special rack. This way they drain rapidly and are completely dry in about half an hour. Do not try to dry them on a heated dryer meant for bromide papers. They will melt!

Contrast variations will be obvious, even with subjects containing few tones. Only the middle one here is correct. The top one is too contrasty, and the bottom one too soft.

Making the colour print

It is difficult to do justice to colour printing in a few words. You will find entire books written on the subject and, even then, they do not cover all the aspects of this arm of darkroom work. Nevertheless, this overview will tell you something of what is involved and help to get you started.

It is possible to use your 'black and white' enlarger. Modern ones have special facilities for adapting to colour use. They either have a drawer for filters, or an alternative head which can be bought separately and which contains the filters already.

Of course, you do need a special set of filters in order to be able to print colour. Remember that you will rarely have the

127

Prints need washing properly, as in this Paterson high speed print washer, to avoid the ultimate presence of stains, and to ensure a permanent picture.

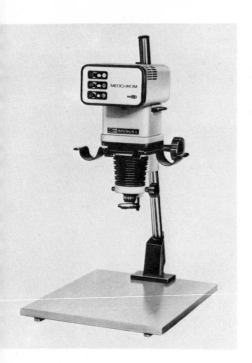

Opemus enlarger with colour head in place.

opportunities to shoot under ideal conditions and your colour negative is likely to be slightly – if not more – out of 'balance'. Add to this processing problems (temperature, agitation, dilution may have been slightly off), enlarger lighting is far from ideal, and so on.

All of these things help to change the colour mix on the film and, if printed directly, would give you all sorts of odd colour casts on your picture. Filters counteract all this.

Additive or subtractive

There are two systems – additive and subtractive. Additive filters are red, blue, and green. You need only one of each and you find the correct balance by exposing through each one separately, at different exposure times. The more popular is the subtractive system. This is surprising at first glance, since you require some 24 filters. However, when you have discovered which filters to use, you can make one exposure through all that is necessary.

Just about every colour enlarger, or colour head, available uses the subtractive system. In these enlargers the filters are not separate entities, but a continuously variable system. You can dial in the filter mix you desire. Separate filters for use in the black and white enlarger's colour drawer are not quite so versatile but they are nevertheless extremely workable. They do not affect the quality of the lens as long as they can be fitted above it. If your enlarger has a drawer, it will be situated just below the bulb. If not, you will have to fit the filters on a special clip which is fitted below the lens.

As with filters you use on your camera, when you add printing filters together, they reduce the amount of light reaching the printing paper. This means that you must pay attention to the filter factors of each one. Most filter kits include a special dial or calculator which helps you to work out the filter factors for any combination used. Nevertheless, it is wise to confirm those figures by tests before you make any important prints.

128

Even with outdoor pictures, you can expect a straight print to produce colour casts. This is because of a variety of factors which can upset the colour balance from shooting to finished pictures – processing problems, the colour temperature of the enlarger bulb, print processing problems, and so forth. Filters are required during enlarging to put the cast right and to produce proper colours more closely resembling those of the original subject.

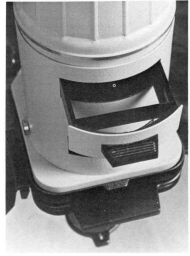

A colour filter drawer in a black and white enlarger.

The Simma-Colour exposure and filter calculator eases colour printing problems.

Any filter kit is suitable for printing negatives or slides. It is the paper you must change. You need a special positive reversal paper to print slides. Once you have that, the method is the same.

Searching for colour

The real difficulties in colour printing lie in working out how to analyse the colour imbalance on the negative, and how to decide which filter pack (mix) you need. There are special electronic analysers available but they are expensive. The idea is to work out the filtration required by tests first, using an average negative, and then as you expose the analyser to each subsequent negative, it will tell you the filter pack to use.

Likewise, the less expensive special filter overlay works the same way. It is laid on the paper and the negative exposed through it. The multitude of filter dots produce a print covered with various shades of grey. These are read carefully to find the neutral tone which matches a key and that is your filtration.

Actually, you can get by without any of these gadgets. All you need to do is make a test strip. This also, gives you the initial information from an average negative which you can then use as a basis for making further prints from the same film.

Bearing this in mind, you can help yourself somewhat by making sure that your exposures during shooting are consistent. Also, standardise on your film and equipment. Use the same materials all the time and you will get to know them so well that they do not require too much thinking about.

A specially designed Durst Comask for producing up to four different prints on the same 10 x 8 in. sheet of printing paper.

All of this will provide the basis for you to be able to use the same filter pack time and time again for the majority of your pictures. And, when there is a difference in the negative, you will know what to do immediately and not have to spend time and money on making further test strips.

Standardise in another way too. Only buy one size of paper. If you stock only 10 x 8 in. paper, you can use it full size or cut it down to convenient half and quarter sizes. To help you with your cut-downs, there are especially designed masking frames. These have four 'doors' and on one piece of paper you can expose up to four different negatives by lifting and exposing through one door at a time. The paper is then processed as a single sheet in the time it normally takes for one picture to be produced.

Processing

A fairly new invention which must be considered as essential is a processing drum. You can develop your colour prints in open trays as you would for black and white but for the sake of economy and ease of use, the drum takes a lot of beating.

Developing a colour print in a Paterson Thermo-Print Drum.

The problem with colour papers is that they are sensitive to all colours. Therefore, you have to work with them in virtual darkness. You cannot use a fairly bright safelight as you would with monochrome.

The colour print processing drum is designed to allow you to process in daylight. It works like the film developing tank. You insert the paper in darkness, close it all down and then switch on the room lights. You then pour in and out the various chemicals with the room light on until the print is fully processed.

Agitation during the various processing stages is important, of course. It must be continuous. This is achieved by rolling the drum back and forth. To hold to the temperature (critical with colour processing), you can do the rolling in a tray of water maintained at the correct temperature.

If you do not use a drum, you will find yourself processing in an open tray under a safelight which is so dim that you might as well be in total darkness. And, since colour processing takes a great deal longer than black and white, that can be uncomfortable.

Moreover, there are more baths to put the print through. Take the negative/positive process, for instance. The steps are:

Development
Bleach-fix
Wash
Stabilisastion
Drying

You might be able to take that but when you decide to make a couple of prints from slides, then you really are in trouble. The time for processing then is extended by more baths.

There are two popular systems, Ektachrome and Cibachrome. The timing for both is about the same, but the number of baths differ enormously. They are:

Ektachrome	Cibachrome
First developer	Developer
Stop bath	
First wash	
Colour developer	
Bleach-fix	Bleach
	Fix
Final wash	Wash
Stabiliser	
Drying	Drying

A colour printing session

Since the subtractive process is virtually universal now we will deal with that only. Assuming also that you have not bought one of the exposure and filtration analysers, the first step is to make a test strip.

Find your best average negative, clean it carefully and thoroughly and place it in the negative carrier in the enlarger. Finally, focus sharply on a spare piece of colour enlarging paper. If you have a focussing magnifier, use that.

The first move you must make is to find the exposure time. This is achieved in exactly the same way as for making a black and white test strip. (Refer to p.124-5 for details.) Process the test strip and read it in a good light. The section which shows the correct density for all the tones/colours in the picture is your proper exposure time.

The next step is to find the correct filter pack. To begin with, you can be sure of needing the UV filter included with your set. It counteracts the strong sensitivity inherent in printing paper to blue.

Your original test strip is your starting point for correcting the inevitable cast. It will show you what that cast is. Wait until it is dry before coming to any firm decisions. Then, to correct it you use the basic rule of choosing a filter or filters of the same colour.

Blue filtration neutralises a blue cast.
Green filtration neutralises a green cast.
Red filtration neutralises a red cast.
Magenta filtration neutralises a magenta cast.
Yellow filtration neutralises a yellow cast.
Cyan filtration neutralises a cyan cast.

Now, it is true that subtractive filters are only available in the so-called complementary colours. To get a primary colour, however, you simply add two of the relevant filters together. Mix equal amounts of magenta and cyan and you get blue – the complementary of the missing colour. Mix yellow and cyan and you end up with green; mix magenta and yellow and you have red.

Even knowing all this, it is still not an easy matter choosing just the right mix of filters to neutralise the cast on the print. You will not always have equal amounts of colour to deal with.

Now comes the confusing bit. To find the way to neutralise the cast you view the print through various combinations of filters of the complementary colour. Thus, if the cast is red, you look at it through various strengths of cyan filters. When

Pick a known colour to get the balance right. If you choose, say, skin tones, you know that if they look right, the other colours should take care of themselves.

you see the correct colour, you know you have the right filtration.

You then revert to filters of the same colour as the cast, for printing through. In this case, you select a mix of magenta and yellow filters.

Should your print cast be magenta, then you mix various individual strengths of yellow and cyan filters (making green) to view through. When you have neutralised the cast, your printing filter must be the same as the cast – magenta.

The trick of this technique is to resist the temptation of staring at the print through your viewing combinations for a long time. That only makes things worse. Glance, instead. Make instant decisions. You will be surprised how often your first choice is very close to the mark.

Now that you have neutralised the cast, you must find the correct strength of filters to use in the enlarger. It must be half the value of the combination through which you viewed. A check on the filter mount, or the packet, will tell you the strength of your viewing filter.

Let us suppose the cast is green and you have neutralised it with a magenta filter with a value of 40. You must now make up a pack of yellow and cyan filters (making green) of half the strength. Thus you choose, 20 cyan and 20 yellow. If, on the other hand, the cast is cyan, and it is neutralised with 30 each of magenta and yellow (to make red), then a 15 cyan is required in the enlarger.

Sadly, colour casts are not usually as obliging as this. Often, you find that they are not pure red, cyan, or anything. They are mixtures of colours requiring sometimes strange combinations to neutralise them. For example, you may find that the cast is neutralised when you view through 10 yellow and 20 magenta.

To work out your enlarging filter pack, you must approach this problem in a slightly different way. Start by taking equal amounts from the two filters – that is, 10 yellow and 10 magenta. Your answer then is 10 red. Therefore, your filter pack, being half that, is 5 cyan (red's complementary colour).

But, that still leaves you with 10 magenta left over.

The answer to that is pretend it is a different filter. Select its complementary colour, green, and halve it. As you make green with cyan and yellow, you now have two more filters with a strength of 5 each. Now, you simply add these to your previously calculated filter pack (5 cyan) to make 10 cyan and 5 yellow.

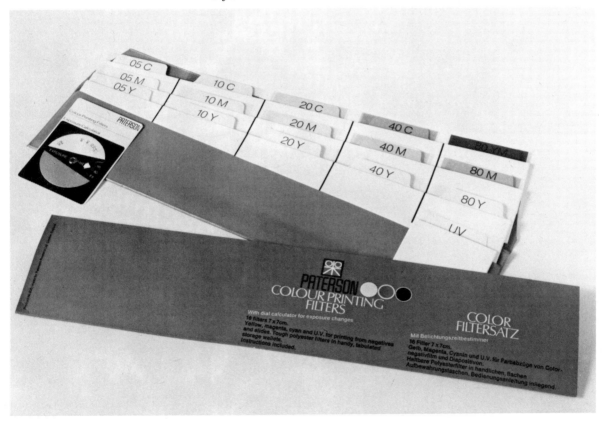

Colour filters meant for printing have filter factors too. They are usually marked on the filter mount and a dial (bottom left corner) tells you what exposure adjustments to make when a filter pack is in place.

All of this sounds complicated but it becomes easier as you fiddle around with filters, and practise it. Like everything else, the more you use a system, the sooner you become familiar, and the easier it is.

Where your calculation ends up giving you values for three different colour filters, stop and reduce them to two. If you print through all three it will take an unnecessarily long

time. All three filters together do is add density. Remember the theories about mixing primary and complementary colours back in the first chapter of this book?

You can remove a filter without altering the balance, provided you reduce the strengths of the remaining two by the same amount as the removed one.

Let us suppose your calculations leave you with 20 yellow, 15 magenta, and 5 cyan. Take away the smallest – cyan – and then reduce the others by 5. That leaves you with 15 yellow and 10 magenta. To repeat, the colour effect will not change but the exposure time will be considerably lessened.

If you have made a mistake with your filter pack and it produces yet another cast, subtract strengths rather than add. If your new cast is green, subtract some magenta – should it be yellow, subtract some cyan and some magenta.

Advance notice

After you have established a standard filter pack for your average negative, you can use a contact sheet to give you advance information about any new films you have shot. Simply make a contact sheet of each new film through your standard filter pack and when it is dry, study it for colour casts.

If you have got everything right, most of your pictures should come out in more or less the proper colours. Some of them, however, will show a distinct cast because you have shot them in lighting which caused the balance to be upset.

When you have identified these, print your correctly balanced ones and then spend time finding the off-balance negatives. Your life will be a whole lot easier in the darkroom if you use this method and, in time, you will recognise exactly what you have to do to correct the cast without having to resort to test strips and the like.

It is true that colour printing is a great deal more finicky than printing in black and white but the end results are well worth it. If you have patience, and have the ability to pay attention to detail, you will do a good job. There are very few short cuts and you have to take things steady.

The important thing is to work at it. If you practise enough, the process will soon speed up and you will have to spend less time over each picture.

Photographs predominantly neutral in tone are particularly difficult to free from colour casts. Careful filtration is needed.

Epilogue

It is so important that we understand this language of photography. If we do, and can use it as proficiently as the spoken word, then we can expect to be successful. Therefore, photography must be practised and the ways and means of using it studied.

This book, hopefully, has helped in this direction, in that you now have the basic rudiments of exercising your new photographic language.

If there is any one rule to follow, it is: never press the button just for the sake of it. Make your pictures communicate. Have them tell some sort of story or express a message. That is, after all, the primary purpose of language. True, the picture is purely a visual means of expressing yourself. But, they say one picture is as good as a thousand words. Therefore, you can make it work wonders. Every picture you take can be made to say something.

If you stay at the snapshooting level because applying some of the 'grammar' of photography is difficult in the beginning, your message will be very basic and be of interest to very few people. If the person looking at your picture was not there with you when you shot it, he is not likely to remain interested for very long. If he shows any emotion at all it is likely to be only out of politeness.

Of course, if the scene you have photographed was prompted by an emotional experience you had at the time, then it is difficult to tell anyone about it. No form of language is adequate. Have you ever tried to tell someone about a funny event in a film or a television programme? It never comes out as funny to you, let alone to the people you are describing it to. Pictures can be like that too. They do, however, rise above that and go a long way towards expressing your feelings if you make them more than just a boost to a personal fond memory. Anything less and they are likely to fade along with the memories. In a year or two's time, you may even wonder why you took that picture at all.

Thus, your pictures must be made to appeal on several levels. Selection of subject is one way. If the viewer can identify with the subject, he will like your picture. For example, mothers like babies; outdoor types love sports; and so on. But, even then, these things can only be a part of your message. You cannot always be around when exciting things are happening to familiar subjects. What is worse, people will often ignore the picture and say things like: 'What a lovely baby', rather than: 'What a lovely picture of a baby'.

So, to stop the photograph becoming a substitute for the real thing, it is necessary to look beyond the normal things

Look for the unusual. When you can see in the most unlikely subjects possible photographs, you are beginning to develop a special and personal photographic vision.

which everyone takes pictures of anyway. We need to find subjects which are different. They might never have been photographed before, and may never be again. It just so happens that all the elements which make the picture came together just at the right time – when you were there.

Thus, you are moved by the special relationship of tones, shapes, colours, or whatever in a most unlikely subject. Sometimes these things happen in a likely subject and you find yourself making a unique picture of ordinary, everyday things. The important thing is, you are creating. You are making something out of virtually nothing.

Your pictures then, move on to express the beauty of the moment and you find unique ways of transferring these things onto film.

It might be a line of washing which catches your eye. As a

photograph, a line of washing seems to be no subject at all. But, then the lighting catches it in a special way, the wind whips the clothes into eerie shapes and suddenly they become a special picture.

On the other hand, you might be impressed by the way a number of roofs 'fall' together. The resultant pattern arrangement can be emphasised with a telephoto lens and you have a remarkable, and very personal, picture.

This is not meant to imply that you should now ignore the more general subjects like babies, sports, scenery, and so on. Rather, it means that you are developing an eye for pictorial arrangement, and colour interplay – in short, vision.

Develop it. Study the points made in this book about putting a picture together to make it express something. Apply them and then feel something about the subjects you shoot. Only then can you work them together to establish ways of expressing those feelings through your camera.

Remember that the picture is made before you press the shutter release button. After you have fired the shutter, it is too late. Get it right in the viewfinder first.

So, after you have read this book, then what? Read it again. Make the points made in these pages work for you. Mere reading is not going to produce a better photographer out of you. Practise the methods until they become second nature to you.

Study other people's pictures too. Not every one you see will appeal to you. That is because photography is a very personal form of communication. Nevertheless, study them. Try to work out what the cameraman is trying to say and how he did it. Wherever possible make a picture of your own copying the expert's. You will learn a great deal that way.

Go to it then. Study photography but enjoy yourself while doing it. If your pictures only appeal to yourself at first, do not let it worry you. Keep on working at it until you can be sure that the people who say, 'What a nice picture!' actually mean it.

Good luck.

Publications
for
photographers

There is no shortage of publications for photographers, as you can see if you look through the magazines at your local newsagents'. In addition to magazines published in Britain, you may find one or two from the U.S.A. Most photography magazines contain advice about photographic techniques, different cameras, film and equipment – and a very large quantity of advertisements. The following are just a small selection of British magazines.

Amateur Photographer
British Journal of Photography
Photo Technique
Photography
Practical Photography
SLR Camera
You and Your Camera

Books on photography are like the magazines: there are a lot of them. These are just a few of the books you can find in your local library or bookshop.

Suzanne Beedell, *The Amateur's Guide to Leisure Photography* (Bartholomew, 1975)
John Hedgecoe, *The Photographer's Handbook* (Ebury Press)
Michael Langford, *The Step by Step Guide to Photography* (Ebury Press)
Peter Marmoy, *Simple Photography (with and without a camera)* (Studio Vista, 1976)
Aaron Sussman, *The Amateur's Handbook* (Crowell, 1941). *This book has now run into several editions.*
John Wasley, *Beginner's Guide to Photography* (Pelham books, Beginner's Guide series, 1973)